# COLLECTED WORKS OF
# EDNA ST. VINCENT MILLAY

# COLLECTED WORKS OF EDNA ST. VINCENT MILLAY

Aria da Capo,
A Few Figs from Thistles,
Second April, and
Renascence and Other Poems

BIBLIOBAZAAR

# COLLECTED WORKS OF
# EDNA ST. VINCENT MILLAY

# CONTENTS

# Life and Times of Millay

1892 – 1950 – Born in Rockland, Maine

1893 – Stock Market crash – Lizzie Borden cleared of murdering her parents Why? No one could believe a shy retiring woman could commit such a crime.

1895 – "GAY Nineties" age of the super rich Joseph Pulitzer, William Vanderbilt, Andrew Carnegie. They had the money but longed for the prestige enjoyed by European aristocrats and landed gentry. So their daughters had penniless but posh husbands purchased for them. female commodities

1896 – Utah finally Joins the Union as 45th state. Radiation used in the treatment of breast cancer.
people started going to "the flicks" as early movies were called

1897 – Louisiana legalises prostitution
major gold strike in Yukon

1898 – Weeping Hawaiian Islanders became a U.S. state
Spanish-American War – 289 lives lost in battle, 4,000 lost to disease. Cuba not safe for outsiders

1900 – Huge immigration swells U.S. population

1901 – Planters in Georgia still holding slaves children sold to the Textile industry in N.Y. worked for 25¢ per day. Roosevelt refused to listen to Labor Leader "Mother Jones"

1904 – huge Italian Immigration

1905 – Vice Squad closes G.B.S. play Mrs Warren's profession

1907 – Oklahoma becomes a state

1912 – Women gain the right to vote in 8 more states in a painfully slow process because of corruption. (A 796 loss wass turned into a 100,000 gain on the second count!) Michigan. Only 9 states gave suffrage in 1914! When Edna was 22

June 1917 – U.S. enters war

Nov 11 1918 – Armistice signed

1920 – Prohibition

# ARIA DA CAPO

## A PLAY IN ONE ACT

PERSONS

> Pierrot
> Columbine
> Cothurnus, Masque of Tragedy
> Thyrsis-\
>       Shepherds
> Corydon-/

[Scene: A stage]

[The curtain rises on a stage set for a Harlequinade, a merry black and white interior. Directly behind the footlights, and running parallel with them, is a long table, covered with a gay black and white cloth, on which is spread a banquet. At the opposite ends of this table, seated on delicate thin-legged chairs with high backs, are Pierrot and Columbine, dressed according to the tradition, excepting that Pierrot is in lilac, and Columbine in pink. They are dining.]

COLUMBINE: Pierrot, a macaroon! I cannot *live* without a macaroon!

PIERROT: My only love, You are *so* intense! . . . Is it Tuesday, Columbine?—I'll kiss you if it's Tuesday.

COLUMBINE: It is Wednesday, If you must know . . . Is this my artichoke, Or yours?

PIERROT: Ah, Columbine,—as if it mattered! Wednesday . . . Will it be Tuesday, then, tomorrow, By any chance?

COLUMBINE: Tomorrow will be—Pierrot, That isn't funny!

PIERROT: I thought it rather nice. Well, let us drink some wine and lose our heads And love each other.

9

COLUMBINE: Pierrot, don't you love Me now?

PIERROT: La, what a woman!—how should I know? Pour me some wine: I'll tell you presently.

COLUMBINE: Pierrot, do you know, I think you drink too much.

PIERROT: Yes, I dare say I do . . . Or else too little. It's hard to tell. You see, I am always wanting A little more than what I have,—or else A little less. There's something wrong. My dear, How many fingers have you?

COLUMBINE: La, indeed, How should I know?—It always takes me one hand To count the other with. It's too confusing. Why?

PIERROT: Why?—I am a student, Columbine; And search into all matters.

COLUMBINE: La, indeed?—Count them yourself, then!

PIERROT: No. Or, rather, nay. 'Tis of no consequence . . . I am become A painter, suddenly,—and you impress me—Ah, yes!—six orange bull's-eyes, four green pin-wheels, And one magenta jelly-roll,—the title As follows: Woman Taking in Cheese from Fire-Escape.

COLUMBINE: Well, I like that! So that is all I've meant To you!

PIERROT: Hush! All at once I am become A pianist. I will image you in sound . . . On a new scale . . ., Without tonality . . . Vivace senza tempo senza tutto . . . Title: Uptown Express at Six O'Clock. Pour me a drink.

COLUMBINE: Pierrot, you work too hard. You need a rest. Come on out into the garden, And sing me something sad.

PIERROT: Don't stand so near me! I am become a socialist. I love Humanity; but I hate people. Columbine, Put on your mittens, child; your hands are cold.

COLUMBINE: My hands are *not* cold!

PIERROT: Oh, I am sure they are. And you must have a shawl to wrap about you, And sit by the fire.

COLUMBINE: Why, I'll do no such thing! I'm hot as a spoon in a teacup!

PIERROT: Columbine, I'm a philanthropist. I know I am, Because I feel so restless. Do not scream, Or it will be the worse for you!

COLUMBINE: Pierrot, My vinaigrette! I cannot *live* without My vinaigrette!

PIERROT: My only love, you are *So* fundamental! . . . How would you like to be An actress, Columbine?—I am become Your manager.

COLUMBINE: Why, Pierrot, *I* can't act.

PIERROT: Can't act! Can't act! La, listen to the woman! What's that to do with the price of furs?—You're blonde, Are you not?— you have no education, have you?—Can't act! You underrate yourself, my dear!

COLUMBINE: Yes, I suppose I do.

PIERROT: As for the rest, I'll teach you how to cry, and how to die, And other little tricks; and the house will love you. You'll be a star by five o'clock . . . that is, If you will let me pay for your apartment.

COLUMBINE: *Let* you?—well, that's a good one! Ha! Ha! Ha! But why?

PIERROT: But why?—well, as to that, my dear, I cannot say. It's just a matter of form.

COLUMBINE: Pierrot, I'm getting tired of caviar And peacocks' livers. Isn't there something else That people eat?—some humble vegetable, That grows in the ground?

PIERROT: Well, there are mushrooms.

COLUMBINE: Mushrooms! That's so! I had forgotten . . . mushrooms . . . mushrooms . . . I cannot *live* with . . . How do you like this gown?

PIERROT: Not much. I'm tired of gowns that have the waist-line About the waist, and the hem around the bottom,—And women with their breasts in front of them!—Zut and ehe! Where does one go from here!

COLUMBINE: Here's a persimmon, love. You always liked them.

PIERROT: I am become a critic; there is nothing I can enjoy . . . However, set it aside; I'll eat it between meals.

COLUMBINE: Pierrot, do you know, Sometimes I think you're making fun of me.

PIERROT: My love, by yon black moon, you wrong us both.

COLUMBINE: There isn't a sign of a moon, Pierrot.

PIERROT: Of course not. There never was. "Moon's" just a word to swear by. "Mutton!"—now *there's* a thing you can lay the hands on, And set the tooth in! Listen, Columbine: I always lied about the moon and you. Food is my only lust.

COLUMBINE: Well, eat it, then, For Heaven's sake, and stop your silly noise! I haven't heard the clock tick for an hour.

PIERROT: It's ticking all the same. If you were a fly, You would be dead by now. And if I were a parrot, I could be talking for a thousand years!

[Enter COTHURNUS.]

PIERROT: Hello, what's this, for God's sake?—What's the matter? Say, whadda you mean?—get off the stage, my friend, And pinch yourself,—you're walking in your sleep!

COTHURNUS: I never sleep.

PIERROT: Well, anyhow, clear out. You don't belong on here. Wait for your own scene! Whadda you think this is,—a dress-rehearsal?

COTHURNUS: Sir, I am tired of waiting. I will wait No longer.

PIERROT: Well, but whadda you going to do? The scene is set for me!

COTHURNUS: True, sir; yet I Can play the scene.

PIERROT: Your scene is down for later!

COTHURNUS: That, too, is true, sir; but I play it now.

PIERROT: Oh, very well!—Anyway, I am tired Of black and white. At least, I think I am.

[Exit COLUMBINE.]

Yes, I am sure I am. I know what I'll do!—I'll go and strum the moon, that's what I'll do . . . Unless, perhaps . . . you never can tell . . . I may be, You know, tired of the moon. Well, anyway, I'll go find Columbine . . . And when I find her, I will address her thus: "Ehe, Pierrette!"—There's something in that.

[Exit PIERROT.]

COTHURNUS: You, Thyrsis! Corydon! Where are you?

THYRSIS: [Off stage.] Sir, we are in our dressing-room!

COTHURNUS: Come out and do the scene.

CORYDON: [Off stage.] You are mocking us!—The scene is down for later.

COTHURNUS: That is true; But we will play it now. I am the scene. [Seats himself on high place in back of stage.]

[Enter CORYDON and THYRSIS.]

CORYDON: Sir, we are counting on this little hour. We said, "Here is an hour,—in which to think A mighty thought, and sing a trifling song, And look at nothing."—And, behold! the hour, Even as we spoke, was over, and the act begun, Under our feet!

THYRSIS: Sir, we are not in the fancy To play the play. We had thought to play it later.

CORYDON: Besides, this is the setting for a farce. Our scene requires a wall; we cannot build A wall of tissue-paper!

THYRSIS: We cannot act A tragedy with comic properties!

COTHURNUS: Try it and see. I think you'll find you can. One wall is like another. And regarding The matter of your insufficient mood, The important thing is that you speak the lines, And make the gestures. Wherefore I shall remain Throughout, and hold the prompt-book. Are you ready?

CORYDON-THYRSIS: [Sorrowfully.] Sir, we are always ready.

COTHURNUS: Play the play!

[CORYDON and THYRSIS move the table and chairs to one side out of the way, and seat themselves in a half-reclining position on the floor.]

THYRSIS: How gently in the silence, Corydon, Our sheep go up the bank. They crop a grass That's yellow where the sun is out, and black Where the clouds drag their shadows. Have you noticed How steadily, yet with what a slanting eye They graze?

CORYDON: As if they thought of other things. What say you, Thyrsis, do they only question Where next to pull?—Or do their far minds draw them Thus vaguely north of west and south of east?

THYRSIS: One cannot say . . . The black lamb wears its burdocks As if they were a garland,—have you noticed? Purple and white—and drinks the bitten grass As if it were a wine.

CORYDON: I've noticed that. What say you, Thyrsis, shall we make a song About a lamb that thought himself a shepherd?

THYRSIS: Why, yes!—that is, why,—no. (I have forgotten my line.)

COTHURNUS: [Prompting.] "I know a game worth two of that!"

THYRSIS: Oh, yes . . . I know a game worth two of that! Let's gather rocks, and build a wall between us; And say that over there belongs to me, And over here to you!

CORYDON: Why,—very well. And say you may not come upon my side Unless I say you may!

THYRSIS: Nor you on mine! And if you should, 'twould be the worse for you!

[They weave a wall of colored crepe paper ribbons from the centre front to the centre back of the stage, fastening the ends to COLUMBINE'S chair in front and to PIERROT'S chair in the back.]

CORYDON: Now there's a wall a man may see across, But not attempt to scale.

THYRSIS: An excellent wall.

CORYDON: Come, let us separate, and sit alone A little while, and lay a plot whereby We may outdo each other. [They seat themselves on opposite sides of the wall.]

PIERROT: [Off stage.] Ehe, Pierrette!

COLUMBINE: [Off stage.] My name is Columbine! Leave me alone!

THYRSIS: [Coming up to the wall.] Corydon, after all, and in spite of the fact I started it myself, I do not like this So very much. What is the sense of saying I do not want you on my side the wall? It is a silly game. I'd much prefer Making the little song you spoke of making, About the lamb, you know, that thought himself A shepherd!—what do you say?

[Pause.]

CORYDON: [At wall.] (I have forgotten the line.)

COTHURNUS: [Prompting.] "How do I know this isn't a trick?"

CORYDON: Oh, yes . . . How do I know this isn't a trick To get upon my land?

THYRSIS: Oh, Corydon, You *know* it's not a trick. I do not like The game, that's all. Come over here, or let me Come over there.

CORYDON: It is a clever trick To get upon my land. [Seats himself as before.]

THYRSIS: Oh, very well! [Seats himself as before.] [To himself.] I think I never knew a sillier game.

CORYDON: [Coming to wall.] Oh, Thyrsis, just a minute!—all the water Is on your side the wall, and the sheep are thirsty. I hadn't thought of that.

THYRSIS: Oh, hadn't you?

CORYDON: Why, what do you mean?

THYRSIS: What do I mean?—I mean That I can play a game as well as you can. And if the pool is on my side, it's on My side, that's all.

CORYDON: You mean you'd let the sheep Go thirsty?

THYRSIS: Well, they're not my sheep. My sheep Have water enough.

CORYDON: *Your* sheep! You are mad, to call them Yours— mine—they are all one flock! Thyrsis, you can't mean To keep the water from them, just because They happened to be grazing over here Instead of over there, when we set the wall up?

THYRSIS: Oh, can't I?—wait and see!—and if you try To lead them over here, you'll wish you hadn't!

CORYDON: I wonder how it happens all the water Is on your side . . . I'll say you had an eye out For lots of little things, my innocent friend, When I said, "Let us make a song," and you said, "I know a game worth two of that!"

COLUMBINE: [Off stage.] Pierrot, D'you know, I think you must be getting old, Or fat, or something,—stupid, anyway!—Can't you put on some other kind of collar?

THYRSIS: You know as well as I do, Corydon, I never thought anything of the kind. *Don't* you?

CORYDON: I *do* not.

THYRSIS: Don't you?

CORYDON: Oh, I suppose so. Thyrsis, let's drop this,—what do you say?—it's only A game, you know . . . we seem to be forgetting It's only a game . . . a pretty serious game It's getting to be, when one of us is willing To let the sheep go thirsty for the sake of it.

THYRSIS: I know it, Corydon.

[They reach out their arms to each other across the wall.]

COTHURNUS: [Prompting.] "But how do I know—"

THYRSIS: Oh, yes . . . But how do I know this isn't a trick To water
your sheep, and get the laugh on me?

CORYDON: You can't know, that's the difficult thing about it, Of
course,—you can't be sure. You have to take My word for it.
And I know just how you feel. But one of us has to take a risk,
or else, Why, don't you see?—the game goes on forever! . . .
It's terrible, when you stop to think of it . . . Oh, Thyrsis, now
for the first time I feel This wall is actually a wall, a thing Come
up between us, shutting you away From me . . . I do not know
you any more!

THYRSIS: No, don't say that! Oh, Corydon, I'm willing To drop
it all, if you will! Come on over And water your sheep! It is an
ugly game. I hated it from the first . . . How did it start?

CORYDON: I do not know . . . I do not know . . . I think I am
afraid of you!—you are a stranger! I never set eyes on you
before! "Come over And water my sheep," indeed!—They'll
be more thirsty Than they are now before I bring them over
Into your land, and have you mixing them up With yours, and
calling them yours, and trying to keep them!

[Enter COLUMBINE]

COLUMBINE: [To COTHURNUS.] Glummy, I want my hat.

THYRSIS: Take it, and go.

COLUMBINE: Take it and go, indeed. Is it my hat, Or isn't it? Is
this my scene, or not? Take it and go! Really, you know, you two
Are awfully funny!

[Exit COLUMBINE]

THYRSIS: Corydon, my friend, I'm going to leave you now, and
whittle me A pipe, or sing a song, or go to sleep. When you
have come to your senses, let me know. [Goes back to where
he has been sitting, lies down and sleeps.]

[CORYDON, in going back to where he has been sitting, stumbles over bowl of colored confetti and colored paper ribbons.]

CORYDON: Why, what is this?—Red stones—and purple stones—And stones stuck full of gold!—The ground is full Of gold and colored stones! . . . I'm glad the wall Was up before I found them!—Otherwise, I should have had to share them. As it is, They all belong to me . . . Unless—

[He goes to wall and digs up and down the length of it, to see if there are jewels on the other side.]

None here—None here—none here—They all belong to me! [Sits.]

THYRSIS: [Awakening.] How curious! I thought the little black lamb Came up and licked my hair; I saw the wool About its neck as plain as anything! It must have been a dream. The little black lamb Is on the other side of the wall, I'm sure.

[Goes to wall and looks over. CORYDON is seated on the ground, tossing the confetti up into the air and catching it.]

Hello, what's that you've got there, Corydon?

CORYDON: Jewels.

THYRSIS: Jewels?—And where did you ever get them?

CORYDON: Oh, over here.

THYRSIS: You mean to say you found them, By digging around in the ground for them?

CORYDON: [Unpleasantly.] No, Thyrsis, By digging down for water for my sheep.

THYRSIS: Corydon, come to the wall a minute, will you? I want to talk to you.

CORYDON: I haven't time. I'm making me a necklace of red stones.

THYRSIS: I'll give you all the water that you want, For one of those red stones,—if it's a good one.

CORYDON: Water?—what for?—what do I want of water?

THYRSIS: Why, for your sheep!

CORYDON: My sheep?—I'm not a shepherd!

THYRSIS: Your sheep are dying of thirst.

CORYDON: Man, haven't I told you I can't be bothered with a few untidy Brown sheep all full of burdocks?—I'm a merchant. That's what I am!—And if I set my mind to it I dare say I could be an emperor! [To himself.] Wouldn't I be a fool to spend my time Watching a flock of sheep go up a hill, When I have these to play with?—when I have these To think about?—I can't make up my mind Whether to buy a city, and have a thousand Beautiful girls to bathe me, and be happy Until I die, or build a bridge, and name it The Bridge of Corydon,—and be remembered After I'm dead.

THYRSIS: Corydon, come to the wall, Won't you?—I want to tell you something.

CORYDON: Hush! Be off! Be off! Go finish your nap, I tell you!

THYRSIS: Corydon, listen: if you don't want your sheep, Give them to me.

CORYDON: Be off! Go finish your nap. A red one—and a blue one—and a red one—And a purple one—give you my sheep, did you say?—Come, come! What do you take me for, a fool? I've a lot of thinking to do,—and while I'm thinking, The sheep might just as well be over here As over there . . . A blue one—and a red one—

THYRSIS: But they will die!

CORYDON: And a green one—and a couple Of white ones, for a change.

THYRSIS: Maybe I have Some jewels on my side.

CORYDON: And another green one—Maybe, but I don't think so. You see, this rock Isn't so very wide. It stops before It gets to the wall. It seems to go quite deep, However.

THYRSIS: [With hatred.] I see.

COLUMBINE: [Off stage.] Look, Pierrot, there's the moon.

PIERROT: [Off stage.] Nonsense!

THYRSIS: I see.

COLUMBINE: [Off stage.] Sing me an old song, Pierrot,—Something I can remember.

PIERROT: [Off stage.] Columbine. Your mind is made of crumbs,—like an escallop Of oysters,—first a layer of crumbs, and then An oystery taste, and then a layer of crumbs.

THYRSIS: [Searching.] I find no jewels . . . but I wonder what The root of this black weed would do to a man If he should taste it. . . . I have seen a sheep die, With half the stalk still drooling from its mouth. 'Twould be a speedy remedy, I should think, For a festered pride and a feverish ambition. It has a curious root. I think I'll hack it In little pieces . . . First I'll get me a drink; And then I'll hack that root in little pieces As small as dust, and see what the color is Inside. [Goes to bowl on floor.]

The pool is very clear. I see A shepherd standing on the brink, with a red cloak About him, and a black weed in his hand . . . 'Tis I. [Kneels and drinks.]

CORYDON: [Coming to wall.] Hello, what are you doing, Thyrsis?

THYRSIS: Digging for gold.

CORYDON: I'll give you all the gold You want, if you'll give me a bowl of water. If you don't want too much, that is to say.

THYRSIS: Ho, so you've changed your mind?—It's different, Isn't it, when you want a drink yourself?

CORYDON: Of course it is.

THYRSIS: Well, let me see . . . a bowl Of water,—come back in an hour, Corydon. I'm busy now.

CORYDON: Oh, Thyrsis, give me a bowl Of water!—and I'll fill the bowl with jewels, And bring it back!

THYRSIS: Be off, I'm busy now.

[He catches sight of the weed, picks it up and looks at it, unseen by CORYDON.]

Wait!—Pick me out the finest stones you have . . . I'll bring you a drink of water presently.

CORYDON: [Goes back and sits down, with the jewels before him.] A bowl of jewels is a lot of jewels.

THYRSIS: [Chopping up the weed.] I wonder if it has a bitter taste.

CORYDON: There's sure to be a stone or two among them I have grown fond of, pouring them from one hand Into the other.

THYRSIS: I hope it doesn't taste Too bitter, just at first.

CORYDON: A bowl of jewels Is far too many jewels to give away And not get back again.

THYRSIS: I don't believe He'll notice. He's too thirsty. He'll gulp it down And never notice.

CORYDON: There ought to be some way To get them back again . . . I could give him a necklace, And snatch it back, after I'd drunk the water, I suppose . . . Why, as for that, of course a *necklace* . . .

[He puts two or three of the colored tapes together and tries their strength by pulling them, after which he puts them around his neck and pulls them, gently, nodding to himself. He gets up and goes to the wall, with the colored tapes in his hands.]

[THYRSIS in the meantime has poured the powdered root—black confetti—into the pot which contained the flower and filled it up with wine from the punch-bowl on the floor. He comes to the wall at the same time, holding the bowl of poison.]

THYRSIS: Come, get your bowl of water, Corydon.

CORYDON: Ah, very good!—and for such a gift as that I'll give you more than a bowl of unset stones. I'll give you three long necklaces, my friend. Come closer. Here they are. [Puts the ribbons about THYRSIS' neck.]

THYRSIS: [Putting bowl to CORYDON'S mouth.] I'll hold the bowl Until you've drunk it all.

CORYDON: Then hold it steady. For every drop you spill I'll have a stone back Out of this chain.

THYRSIS: I shall not spill a drop.

[CORYDON drinks, meanwhile beginning to strangle THYRSIS.]

THYRSIS: Don't pull the string so tight.

CORYDON: You're spilling the water.

THYRSIS: You've had enough—you've had enough—stop pulling The string so tight!

CORYDON: Why, that's not tight at all . . . How's this?

THYRSIS: [Drops bowl.] You're strangling me! Oh, Corydon! It's only a game!—and you are strangling me!

CORYDON: It's only a game, is it?—Yet I believe You've poisoned me in earnest! [Writhes and pulls the strings tighter, winding them about THYRSIS' neck.]

THYRSIS: Corydon! [Dies.]

CORYDON: You've poisoned me in earnest . . . I feel so cold . . . So cold . . . this is a very silly game . . . Why do we play it?— let's not play this game A minute more . . . let's make a little song About a lamb . . . I'm coming over the wall, No matter what you say,—I want to be near you . . .

[Groping his way, with arms wide before him, he strides through the frail papers of the wall without knowing it, and continues seeking for the wall straight across the stage.]

Where is the wall?

[Gropes his way back, and stands very near THYRSIS without seeing him; he speaks slowly.]

There isn't any wall,
I think.

[Takes a step forward, his foot touches THYRSIS' body, and he falls down beside him.]

Thyrsis, where is your cloak?—just give me
A little bit of your cloak! . . .

[Draws corner of THYRSIS' cloak over his shoulders, falls across THYRSIS' body, and dies.]

[COTHURNUS closes the prompt-book with a bang, arises matter-of-factly, comes down stage, and places the table over the two bodies, drawing down the cover so that they are hidden from any actors on the stage, but visible to the audience, pushing in their feet and hands with his boot. He then turns his back to the audience, and claps his hands twice.]

COTHURNUS: Strike the scene! [Exit COTHURNUS.]

[Enter PIERROT and COLUMBINE.]

PIERROT: Don't puff so, Columbine!

COLUMBINE: Lord, what a mess This set is in! If there's one thing I hate Above everything else,—even more than getting my feet wet—It's clutter!—He might at least have left the scene The way he found it . . . don't you say so, Pierrot?

[She picks up punch bowl. They arrange chairs as before at ends of table.]

PIERROT: Well, I don't know. I think it rather diverting The way it is.

[Yawns, picks up confetti bowl.]

Shall we begin?

COLUMBINE: [Screams.] My God! What's that there under the table?

PIERROT: It is the bodies Of the two shepherds from the other play.

COLUMBINE: [Slowly.] How curious to strangle him like that, With colored paper ribbons.

PIERROT: Yes, and yet I dare say he is just as dead. [Pauses. Calls.] Cothurnus! Come drag these bodies out of here! We can't Sit down and eat with two dead bodies lying Under the table! . . . The audience wouldn't stand for it!

COTHURNUS: (Off stage.) What makes you think so?—Pull down the tablecloth On the other side, and hide them from the house, And play the farce. The audience will forget.

PIERROT: That's so. Give me a hand there, Columbine.

[PIERROT and COLUMBINE pull down the table cover in such a way that the two bodies are hidden from the house, then merrily set their bowls back on the table, draw up their chairs, and begin the play exactly as before.]

COLUMBINE: Pierrot, a macaroon,—I cannot *live* without a macaroon!

PIERROT: My only love, You are *so* intense! . . . Is it Tuesday, Columbine?—I'll kiss you if it's Tuesday.

[Curtains begin to close slowly.]

COLUMBINE: It is Wednesday, If you must know. . . . Is this my artichoke Or yours?

PIERROT: Ah, Columbine, as if it mattered! Wednesday . . . Will it be Tuesday, then, tomorrow, By any chance? . . .

[CURTAIN.]

AUTHOR'S NOTE
ON THE PLAYING PO
ARIA DA CAPO

# ORIGINAL CAST

AS PLAYED BY THE PROVINCETOWN PLAYERS, NEW YORK CITY

| | |
|---|---|
| PIERROT | HARRISON DOWD |
| COLUMBINE | NORMA MILLAY |
| COTHURNUS | HUGH FERRISS |
| CORYDON | CHARLES ELLIS |
| THYRSIS | JAMES LIGHT |

# AUTHOR'S NOTE

So great is my vexation always, when reading a play, to find its progress constantly being halted and its structure loosened by elaborate explanatory parentheses, that I resolved when I should publish Aria da Capo to incorporate into its text only those explanations the omission of which might confuse the reader or lend a wrong interpretation to the lines. Since, however, Aria da Capo was written not only to be read but also to be acted, and being conscious that the exclusion of the usual directions, while clarifying the play to the reader, may make it bare of suggestions and somewhat baffling to the producer, I am adding here some remarks which have been found of value in preparing it for presentation on the stage.

Since the production of Aria da Capo by the Provincetown Players, I have received a great many letters from the directors of little theatres, asking for copies of it with a view to producing it. Very often, after I send the play, I receive a letter in reply asking for some suggestions for its presentation, and enclosing direct questions on points that have been difficult. It occurred to me finally that it would be reasonable to make up a sort of informal prompt-book to send about with the play; and it is that which is printed below. It will be found incomplete and uneven, in some instances unnecessarily detailed, in others not sufficiently so; all of which is due to the fact that it was put together loosely, from answers to chance questions, rather than logically, as an entity in itself.

# SUGGESTIONS FOR THE PRODUCTION OF "ARIA DA CAPO"

## SETTING:

The setting required is simple:—a grey curtain, a long black table, two slender black high-backed chairs, and a raised platform.

Instead of wings and back-drop the Provincetown Players cleverly utilized painted screens, the heights varying from 6 to 10 feet, these being set right and left of the stage in such manner as to give the effect of depth and distance.

The table, six feet long and two feet wide, has thin legs and is painted black.

When Pierrot and Columbine enter in the final scene, it is not necessary that the table which Cothurnus has replaced shall entirely conceal the bodies of Thyrsis and Corydon. Pierrot and Columbine must ignore them until the lines indicate their discovery, no matter how they may have fallen.

Particular attention must be given to the chairs in this set. They are used to construct the tissue-paper wall, and, although delicate, should be heavy enough to remain solid and steady, up and down stage, without the possibility of an upset when Corydon strides through the wall.

Near the footlights (actors' left) are two sofa pillows, used to represent the rocks against which the shepherds lean. On the left of the stage have another pillow, which Thyrsis places under his head when he lies down to sleep. Use cloth or crepe paper for these pillows, and have them of spotted black and white material, or of any gay color except red or blue.

Cothurnus occupies a chair upon a platform, up-stage, centre, with two or three steps surrounding it on three sides. Drape this with plain heavy black cloth.

The table covering is important. Its width is equal to that of the added height and width of the table. As it must be moved to cover the bodies of Thyrsis and Corydon, it should be of sufficient weight to prevent slipping. It will be well to experiment with this, to ensure proper performance.

The cover should have black and white spots and striped ends.

The table is set as follows:—two large wooden bowls (at least seven inches high and fourteen inches in diameter). One is placed at each end of the table. That at Columbine's end should contain persimmons, pomegranates, grapes and other bright exotic fruits. Pierrot's bowl has confetti and colored paper ribbons, the latter showing plainly over the edge. (If Columbine uses practical macaroons, put them into this bowl.)

Near Columbine, place a practical uncooked artichoke; have this of good size, and nail it to a wooden standard, painted black. At both places there are tall white wooden goblets.

In the centre of the table there should be a curious, grotesque, but very gay flower, standing upright in a pot of wood or heavy paper, which will not break when Thyrsis drops it. Concealed at the root of this plant there should be a small sack of black confetti, to be used in the "poison scene."

The table should be set with nothing but these articles, and yet give the appearance of bounty and elegance.

Place the table parallel with the footlights,—the long side toward the audience.

Columbine's chair is at the actors' right, and Pierrot's opposite—Columbine's hat hangs from her chair-top. Both chairs are festooned with tissue-paper ribbons, at least ten feet long, to be used later by the shepherds to represent their wall. These must be of such a texture as to break readily when Corydon walks through, and a prearranged transverse tear or two will assist in the prompt breakage when he does so.

## PROPERTIES:

Two white wooden bowls, one filled with fruits and the other with confetti and paper ribbons,—one ribbon to be of cotton or silk, in order to be not too easily broken by Corydon when strangling Thyrsis

Two tall white wooden goblets

One artichoke nailed to a standard

One flower in paper or wooden pot, the root wrapped with black crepe paper (or use confetti)

Black and white tablecloth

Macaroons

Boots and prompt-book for Cothurnus (large flat black book)

Also, if desired, mask of Tragedy for Cothurnus

Crepe or tissue streamers of different colors, including no red or blue, for wall.

## COSTUMES:

PIERROT: Lavender or lilac satin, preferably a blue-lavender. Care should be taken that the lavender does not turn pink under the stage lights. Pierrot's costume is the conventional smock with wide trousers, with black crepe paper rosettes on the smock, wide white tarleton ruff. Black evening pumps with black rosettes may be worn. Black silk skull-cap.

COLUMBINE: Tight black satin bodice cut very low, with straps over the shoulders, quite like the modern evening gown; very full tarleton skirts of different shades of pink and cerise, reaching to the knees; ruffled bloomers of apple-green tarleton, the ruffles showing below the skirts; black silk stockings and black ballet slippers, laced with green. Hat of lavender crepe paper, with streamers of gay colors—including, however, no clear red or blue. Hat should be small and very smart—not a *shepherdess* hat. Columbine should be made up to suggest a doll. As originally interpreted she had short light hair, standing out bushily all over her head. Long hair should be rolled under to give a *bobbed* effect, or could be arranged in obvious caricature of some extreme modern style, but must look attractive, and must be blonde.

COTHURNUS: Plain toga of dull purple in some heavy, unreflecting material which will fall into large folds, lined with sombre flame-color; a garment with large purple sleeves, of which only the sleeves were visible, was worn under the toga,—but the effect should be classical; heavy boots should be worn, as nearly as possible like the tragic Roman buskin; one end of the great toga is tied into a rough hood which covers the actor's head; a mask may be worn, but it is often difficult to speak through, and, if desired, the actor's face may be made up to represent a mask of Tragedy.

THYRSIS and CORYDON: These costumes, in striking contrast to the elegance of those of Pierrot and Columbine, should be very simple, and very roughly made; short tunics of outing-flannel or some such material—fastened loosely over one shoulder,—one shoulder, as well as most of the back and breast, exposed. Legs bare, or swathed from the knee to the ankle in rough strips of the same material. Sandals. Cloaks of heavier, cheap material fastened to the tunics in such a way that they will appear to be simply flung over the shoulder, but actually fastened very cleverly in order to avoid tripping the shepherds, who are continually sitting down on the floor and getting up again.

Thyrsis wears a dark grey tunic and cloak of raw bright red,—but not a turkey-red, as this color will kill the blue of Corydon's cloak. Corydon wears tunic of light grey and cloak of brilliant blue. There must be no red or blue used anywhere in the entire play excepting in the blue and red of these two cloaks. The two shepherds must be so strong and vivid in every way that when Columbine comes in and says, "Is this my scene or not?" it will seem to the audience that it is she, not the shepherds, who is hopelessly out of the scene.

CHARACTERS:

PIERROT: Pierrot sees clearly into existing evils and is rendered gaily cynical by them; he is both too indolent and too indifferent to do anything about it. Yet in several lines of the play his actual unhappiness is seen,—for instance, "Moon's just a word to swear by," in which he expresses his conviction that all beauty and romance are fled from the world. At the end of the play the line, "Yes, and yet I dare say he is just as dead," must not be said flippantly or cynically, but slowly and with much philosophic concentration on the thought. From the moment when Columbine cries, "What's that there under the table?" until Pierrot calls, "Cothurnus, come drag these bodies out of here!" they both stand staring at the two bodies, without moving in any way, or even lifting their eyes. (This same *holding* of the play is used several times also by the shepherds,— for instance, always during the off-stage interpolations, they stand either staring at each other across the wall, or maintaining whatever other position they may have had when the off-stage voice begins speaking, until the interruption is over, when they resume their drama quite as if nobody had spoken.) Columbine's "How curious to strangle him like that" is spoken extremely slowly, in a voice of awe, curiosity, and horror. For a moment the two characters seem almost to feel and be subdued by the tragedy that has taken place. They remain standing very quietly while Cothurnus speaks his final lines off stage, and for a moment after he has said, "The audience will forget"; then very slowly raise their eyes and exchange glances, Pierrot nods his head curtly and says, "That's so"; they set their bowls gaily back on the table, and the play begins again.

Pierrot in such lines as "Ah, Columbine, as if it mattered!" speaks with mock saccharine tenderness; but in such lines as "If you were a fly you would be dead by now!" although he speaks very gaily his malice must be apparent almost even to her; Columbine bores him to death. When he says, "I'll go and strum the moon!" he is for the instant genuinely excited and interested; he is for this moment like a child, and is happy.

COLUMBINE: Pretty and charming, but stupid; she never knows what Pierrot is talking about, and is so accustomed to him that she no longer pretends to understand him; but she is very proud of him, and when he speaks she listens with trustful admiration. Her expression, "I cannot live without" this or that, is a phrase she uses in order to make herself more attractive, because she believes men prefer women to be useless and extravagant; if left to herself she would be a domestic and capable person.

COTHURNUS: This character should be played by a tall and imposing figure with a tremendous voice. The voice of Cothurnus is one of the most important things in the acting play. He should have a voice deeper than the voice used by any of the other persons, should speak weightily and with great dignity, but almost without intonation, and quite without feeling, as if he had said the same words many times before. Only in his last speech may he be permitted a comment on the situation. This speech should be spoken quite as impressively as the others and fully as slowly.

CORYDON and THYRSIS: These two characters are young, very simple, and childlike; they are acted upon by the force that sits on the back of the stage behind them. More and more as their quarrel advances they begin to see that something is wrong, but they have no idea what to do about it, and they scarcely realize what is happening, the quarrel grows so from little things into big things. Corydon's first vision of the tragedy is in "It's terrible when you stop to think of it." Thyrsis' first vision comes when he looks into the pool; in seeing the familiar reflection he is struck by the unfamiliarity of one aspect of it, the poisonous root; for the first time he realizes that this man who is about to kill with poisoned water his most beloved friend, is none other than Thyrsis *himself*,—"'Tis I!" The personalities of Thyrsis and Corydon are not essentially different. They develop somewhat differently, because of the differing circumstances.

When Columbine goes out for the first time she takes with her her artichoke and her wine-glass, also a couple of macaroons, which she nibbles, going out. This helps to get the table cleared. The other articles are removed by the shepherds when they prepare the stage for their scene, in this manner: at the cue "Sir, we are always ready . . . Play the play!", Corydon and Thyrsis come down stage, Corydon to Pierrot's end of the table, Thyrsis to Columbia's; simultaneously, first, they set back the chairs against the wall, Pierrot's left front, Columbine's right front; next they remove the two big bowls and set them in symmetrical positions on the floor, left front and right front, in such a way that the bowl of confetti may be the mine of jewels for Corydon, and the bowl of fruits, the punch-bowl, may represent the pool of water for Thyrsis; then, taking the table by the two ends, they set it back against the wall, right; next, while Corydon places the two pillows from the left wall on the floor to represent rocks in their pasture, Thyrsis removes from the table everything that is left on it except the tablecloth,— this should be only Pierrot's wine-goblet and the flower in its pot. (The flower is to represent later the poisonous weed which Thyrsis finds, the wine-goblet a drinking-cup beside the pool, the flower-pot a bowl in which to mix the poison and bring it to Corydon.) The two shepherds do this setting of their stage swiftly and silently, then seat themselves at once, in easy but beautiful postures, and remain for a moment looking off as if at their sheep while a complete silence settles over the stage and house,—a *pastoral* silence, if it is possible to suggest it—before they begin to speak.

When Columbine comes in, looking for her hat, she picks up the hat from her chair, now in the centre of the stage near the footlights, in a direct line with Pierrot's, which is centre back, just in front of Cothurnus,—the shepherds having set them in these positions, back to back, in order to have their aid in weaving the wall. After taking her hat, Columbine stands looking at the shepherds to see what is going on. They do not look at her. After a moment Thyrsis, slowly, with his eyes steadfastly on Corydon's, says, "Take it, and go." When Columbine comes in in the final scene, she is wearing the hat. She takes it off, however, as she sits down again at the table, so that the second beginning of the play may recall as vividly as possible to the audience the first beginning.

# A FEW FIGS FROM THISTLES

Poems and Sonnets

Thanks are due to the editors of Ainslie's, The Dial, Pearson's Poetry, Reedy's Mirror, and Vanity Fair, for their kind permission to republish various of these poems.

This edition of "A Few Figs from Thistles" contains several poems not included in earlier editions.

## First Fig

My candle burns at both ends;
    It will not last the night ;
But ah, my foes, and oh, my friends—
    It gives a lovely light!

## Second Fig

Safe upon the solid rock the ugly houses stand:
Come and see my shining palace built upon the sand!

## Recuerdo

We were very tired, we were very merry—
We had gone back and forth all night on the ferry.
It was bare and bright, and smelled like a stable—

But we looked into a fire, we leaned across a table,
We lay on a hill-top underneath the moon;
And the whistles kept blowing, and the dawn came soon.

We were very tired, we were very merry—
We had gone back and forth all night on the ferry;
And you ate an apple, and I ate a pear,
From a dozen of each we had bought somewhere;
And the sky went wan, and the wind came cold,
And the sun rose dripping, a bucketful of gold.

We were very tired, we were very merry,
We had gone back and forth all night on the ferry.
We hailed, "Good morrow, mother!" to a shawl-covered head,
And bought a morning paper, which neither of us read;
And she wept, "God bless you!" for the apples and pears,
And we gave her all our money but our subway fares.

## Thursday

And if I loved you Wednesday,
      Well, what is that to you?
I do not love you Thursday—
      So much is true.

And why you come complaining
      Is more than I can see.
I loved you Wednesday,—yes—but what
      Is that to me?

## To the Not Impossible Him

How shall I know, unless I go
      To Cairo and Cathay,
Whether or not this blessed spot
      Is blest in every way?

Now it may be, the flower for me
    Is this beneath my nose;
How shall I tell, unless I smell
    The Carthaginian rose?

The fabric of my faithful love
    No power shall dim or ravel
Whilst I stay here,—but oh, my dear,
    If I should ever travel!

# Macdougal Street

As I went walking up and down to take the evening air,
    (Sweet to meet upon the street, why must I be so shy?)
I saw him lay his hand upon her torn black hair;
    ("Little dirty Latin child, let the lady by!")

The women squatting on the stoops were slovenly and fat,
    (Lay me out in organdie, lay me out in lawn!)
And everywhere I stepped there was a baby or a cat;
    (Lord God in Heaven, will it never be dawn?)

The fruit-carts and clam-carts were ribald as a fair,
    (Pink nets and wet shells trodden under heel)
She had haggled from the fruit-man of his rotting ware;
    (I shall never get to sleep, the way I feel!)

He walked like a king through the filth and the clutter,
    (Sweet to meet upon the street, why did you glance me by?)
But he caught the quaint Italian quip she flung him from the gutter;
    (What can there be to cry about that I should lie and cry?)

He laid his darling hand upon her little black head,
    (I wish I were a ragged child with ear-rings in my ears!)
And he said she was a baggage to have said what she had said;
    (Truly I shall be ill unless I stop these tears!)

# The Singing-Woman from the Wood's Edge

What should I be but a prophet and a liar,
Whose mother was a leprechaun, whose father was a friar?
Teethed on a crucifix and cradled under water,
What should I be but the fiend's god-daughter?

And who should be my playmates but the adder and the frog,
That was got beneath a furze-bush and born in a bog?
And what should be my singing, that was christened at an altar,
But Aves and Credos and Psalms out of the Psalter?

You will see such webs on the wet grass, maybe,
As a pixie-mother weaves for her baby,
You will find such flame at the wave's weedy ebb
As flashes in the meshes of a mer-mother's web,

But there comes to birth no common spawn
From the love of a priest for a leprechaun,
And you never have seen and you never will see
Such things as the things that swaddled me!

After all's said and after all's done,
What should I be but a harlot and a nun?

In through the bushes, on any foggy day,
My Da would come a-swishing of the drops away,
With a prayer for my death and a groan for my birth,
A-mumbling of his beads for all that he was worth.

And there'd sit my Ma, with her knees beneath her chin,
A-looking in his face and a-drinking of it in,
And a-marking in the moss some funny little saying
That would mean just the opposite of all that he was praying!

He taught me the holy-talk of Vesper and of Matin,
He heard me my Greek and he heard me my Latin,

He blessed me and crossed me to keep my soul from evil,
And we watched him out of sight, and we conjured up the devil!

Oh, the things I haven't seen and the things I haven't known.
What with hedges and ditches till after I was grown,
And yanked both ways by my mother and my father,
With a "Which would you better?" and a "Which would you rather?"

With him for a sire and her for a dam,
What should I be but just what I am?

## She Is Overheard Singing

*How women can't help falling for a rogue*

Oh, Prue she has a patient man,
    And Joan a gentle lover,
And Agatha's Arth' is a hug-the-hearth,—
    But my true love's a rover!

Mig, her man's as good as cheese
    And honest as a briar,
Sue tells her love what he's thinking of,—
    But my dear lad's a liar!

Oh, Sue and Prue and Agatha
    Are thick with Mig and Joan!
They bite their threads and shake their heads
    And gnaw my name like a bone;

And Prue says, "Mine's a patient man,
    As never snaps me up,"
And Agatha, "Arth' is a hug-the-hearth,
    Could live content in a cup;"

Sue's man's mind is like good jell—
    All one colour, and clear—
And Mig's no call to think at all
    What's to come next year,

While Joan makes boast of a gentle lad,
    That's troubled with that and this;—
But they all would give the life they live
    For a look from the man I kiss!

Cold he slants his eyes about,
    And few enough's his choice,—
Though he'd slip me clean for a nun, or a queen,
    Or a beggar with knots in her voice,—

And Agatha will turn awake
    While her good man sleeps sound,
And Mig and Sue and Joan and Prue
    Will hear the clock strike round,

For Prue she has a patient man,
    As asks not when or why,
And Mig and Sue have naught to do
    But peep who's passing by,

Joan is paired with a putterer
    That bastes and tastes and salts,
And Agatha's Arth' is a hug-the-hearth,—
    But my true love is false!

## The Prisoner

All right,
Go ahead!
What's in a name?
I guess I'll be locked into
As much as I'm locked out of!

## The Unexplorer

There was a road ran past our house
Too lovely to explore.

I asked my mother once—she said
That if you followed where it led
It brought you to the milk-man's door.
(That's why I have not traveled more.)

## Grown-up

Was it for this I uttered prayers,
And sobbed and cursed and kicked the stairs,
That now, domestic as a plate,
I should retire at half-past eight?

## The Penitent

I had a little Sorrow,
    Born of a little Sin,
I found a room all damp with gloom
    And shut us all within;
And, "Little Sorrow, weep," said I,
    "And, Little Sin, pray God to die,
And I upon the floor will lie
    And think how bad I've been!"

Alas for pious planning—
    It mattered not a whit!
As far as gloom went in that room,
    The lamp might have been lit!
My little Sorrow would not weep,
    My little Sin would go to sleep—
To save my soul I could not keep
    My graceless mind on it!

So up I got in anger,
    And took a book I had,
And put a ribbon on my hair
    To please a passing lad,

And, "One thing there's no getting by—
I've been a wicked girl," said I;
"But if I can't be sorry, why,
    I might as well be glad!"

# Daphne

Why do you follow me?—
Any moment I can be
Nothing but a laurel-tree.

Any moment of the chase
I can leave you in my place
A pink bough for your embrace.

Yet if over hill and hollow
Still it is your will to follow,
I am off;—to heel, Apollo!

# Portrait by a Neighbor

Before she has her floor swept
    Or her dishes done,
Any day you'll find her
    A-sunning in the sun!

It's long after midnight
    Her key's in the lock,
And you never see her chimney smoke
    Till past ten o'clock!

She digs in her garden
    With a shovel and a spoon,
She weeds her lazy lettuce
    By the light of the moon,

She walks up the walk
    Like a woman in a dream,
She forgets she borrowed butter
    And pays you back cream!

Her lawn looks like a meadow,
    And if she mows the place
She leaves the clover standing
    And the Queen Anne's lace!

## Midnight Oil

Cut if you will, with Sleep's dull knife,
    Each day to half its length, my friend,—
The years that Time takes off _my_ life,
    He'll take from off the other end!

## The Merry Maid

Oh, I am grown so free from care
    Since my heart broke!
I set my throat against the air,
    I laugh at simple folk!

There's little kind and little fair
    Is worth its weight in smoke
To me, that's grown so free from care
    Since my heart broke!

Lass, if to sleep you would repair
    As peaceful as you woke,
Best not besiege your lover there
    For just the words he spoke
To me, that's grown so free from care
    Since my heart broke!

## To Kathleen

Still must the poet as of old,
In barren attic bleak and cold,
Starve, freeze, and fashion verses to
Such things as flowers and song and you;

Still as of old his being give
In Beauty's name, while she may live,
Beauty that may not die as long
As there are flowers and you and song.

## To S. M.
### If he should lie a-dying

I am not willing you should go
Into the earth, where Helen went;
She is awake by now, I know.
Where Cleopatra's anklets rust
You will not lie with my consent;
And Sappho is a roving dust;
Cressid could love again; Dido,
Rotted in state, is restless still:
You leave me much against my will.

## The Philosopher

And what are you that, wanting you
    I should be kept awake
As many nights as there are days
    With weeping for your sake?

And what are you that, missing you,
    As many days as crawl

I should be listening to the wind
　　And looking at the wall?

I know a man that's a braver man
　　And twenty men as kind,
And what are you, that you should be
　　The one man in my mind?

Yet women's ways are witless ways,
　　As any sage will tell,—
And what am I, that I should love
　　So wisely and so well?

# Four Sonnets

## I

Love, though for this you riddle me with darts,
And drag me at your chariot till I die,—
Oh, heavy prince! Oh, panderer of hearts!—
Yet hear me tell how in their throats they lie
Who shout you mighty: thick about my hair
Day in, day out, your ominous arrows purr
Who still am free, unto no querulous care
A fool, and in no temple worshiper!
I, that have bared me to your quiver's fire,
Lifted my face into its puny rain,
Do wreathe you Impotent to Evoke Desire
As you are Powerless to Elicit Pain!
(Now will the god, for blasphemy so brave,
Punish me, surely, with the shaft I crave!)

## II

I think I should have loved you presently,
And given in earnest words I flung in jest;
And lifted honest eyes for you to see,

And caught your hand against my cheek and breast;
And all my pretty follies flung aside
That won you to me, and beneath your gaze,
Naked of reticence and shorn of pride,
Spread like a chart my little wicked ways.
I, that had been to you, had you remained,
But one more waking from a recurrent dream,
Cherish no less the certain stakes I gained,
And walk your memory's halls, austere, supreme,
A ghost in marble of a girl you knew
Who would have loved you in a day or two.

*Women are no more* ### III *constant*
*than men*

Oh, think not I am faithful to a vow!
Faithless am I save to love's self alone.
Were you not lovely I would leave you now;
After the feet of beauty fly my own.
Were you not still my hunger's rarest food,
And water ever to my wildest thirst,
I would desert you—think not but I would!—
And seek another as I sought you first.
But you are mobile as the veering air,
And all your charms more changeful than the tide,
Wherefore to be inconstant is no care:
I have but to continue at your side.
So wanton, light and false, my love, are you,
I am most faithless when I most am true.

### IV

I shall forget you presently, my dear,
So make the most of this, your little day,
Your little month, your little half a year,
Ere I forget, or die, or move away, *— continue on*
And we are done forever; by and by
I shall forget you, as I said, but now,
If you entreat me with your loveliest lie
I will protest you with my favorite vow.

I would indeed that love were longer-lived,
And oaths were not so brittle as they are,
But so it is, and nature has contrived
To struggle on without a break thus far,—
Whether or not we find what we are seeking
Is idle, biologically speaking.

Edna had no patience with the
notion: "To a man, love is a thing
apart while to a woman it is her whole
existence."

Women were only faithful if they jolly
well had to be. In her day a woman
was dependant on a man for a roof
over her head and to ~~to~~ put food on
the table.

# SECOND APRIL

TO

MY BELOVED FRIEND

CAROLINE B. DOW

# SPRING

To what purpose, April, do you return again?
Beauty is not enough.
You can no longer quiet me with the redness
Of little leaves opening stickily.
I know what I know.
The sun is hot on my neck as I observe
The spikes of the crocus.
The smell of the earth is good.
It is apparent that there is no death.
But what does that signify?
Not only under ground are the brains of men
Eaten by maggots,
Life in itself
Is nothing,
An empty cup, a flight of uncarpeted stairs.
It is not enough that yearly, down this hill,
April
Comes like an idiot, babbling and strewing flowers.

## CITY TREES

The trees along this city street,
    Save for the traffic and the trains,
Would make a sound as thin and sweet
    As trees in country lanes.

And people standing in their shade
    Out of a shower, undoubtedly

Would hear such music as is made
    Upon a country tree.

Oh, little leaves that are so dumb
    Against the shrieking city air,
I watch you when the wind has come,—
    I know what sound is there.

## THE BLUE-FLAG IN THE BOG

God had called us, and we came;
    Our loved Earth to ashes left;
Heaven was a neighbor's house,
    Open to us, bereft.

Gay the lights of Heaven showed,
    And 'twas God who walked ahead;
Yet I wept along the road,
    Wanting my own house instead.

Wept unseen, unheeded cried,
    "All you things my eyes have kissed,
Fare you well! We meet no more,
    Lovely, lovely tattered mist!

Weary wings that rise and fall
    All day long above the fire!"—
Red with heat was every wall,
    Rough with heat was every wire—

"Fare you well, you little winds
    That the flying embers chase!
Fare you well, you shuddering day,
    With your hands before your face!

And, ah, blackened by strange blight,
    Or to a false sun unfurled,

Now forevermore goodbye,
     All the gardens in the world!

On the windless hills of Heaven,
     That I have no wish to see,
White, eternal lilies stand,
     By a lake of ebony.

But the Earth forevermore
     Is a place where nothing grows,—
Dawn will come, and no bud break;
     Evening, and no blossom close.

Spring will come, and wander slow
     Over an indifferent land,
Stand beside an empty creek,
     Hold a dead seed in her hand."

God had called us, and we came,
     But the blessed road I trod
Was a bitter road to me,
     And at heart I questioned God.

"Though in Heaven," I said, "be all
     That the heart would most desire,
Held Earth naught save souls of sinners
     Worth the saving from a fire?

Withered grass,—the wasted growing!
     Aimless ache of laden boughs!"
Little things God had forgotten
     Called me, from my burning house.

"Though in Heaven," I said, "be all
     That the eye could ask to see,
All the things I ever knew
     Are this blaze in back of me."

"Though in Heaven," I said, "be all
	That the ear could think to lack,
All the things I ever knew
	Are this roaring at my back."

It was God who walked ahead,
	Like a shepherd to the fold;
In his footsteps fared the weak,
	And the weary and the old,

Glad enough of gladness over,
	Ready for the peace to be,—
But a thing God had forgotten
	Was the growing bones of me.

And I drew a bit apart,
	And I lagged a bit behind,
And I thought on Peace Eternal,
	Lest He look into my mind:

And I gazed upon the sky,
	And I thought of Heavenly Rest,—
And I slipped away like water
	Through the fingers of the blest!

All their eyes were fixed on Glory,
	Not a glance brushed over me;
"Alleluia! Alleluia!"
	Up the road,—and I was free.

And my heart rose like a freshet,
	And it swept me on before,
Giddy as a whirling stick,
	Till I felt the earth once more.

All the earth was charred and black,
	Fire had swept from pole to pole;
And the bottom of the sea
	Was as brittle as a bowl;

And the timbered mountain-top
    Was as naked as a skull,—
Nothing left, nothing left,
    Of the Earth so beautiful!

"Earth," I said, "how can I leave you?"
    "You are all I have," I said;
"What is left to take my mind up,
    Living always, and you dead?"

"Speak!" I said, "Oh, tell me something!
    Make a sign that I can see!
For a keepsake! To keep always!
    Quick!—before God misses me!"

And I listened for a voice;—
    But my heart was all I heard;
Not a screech-owl, not a loon,
    Not a tree-toad said a word.

And I waited for a sign;—
    Coals and cinders, nothing more;
And a little cloud of smoke
    Floating on a valley floor.

And I peered into the smoke
    Till it rotted, like a fog:—
There, encompassed round by fire,
    Stood a blue-flag in a bog!

Little flames came wading out,
    Straining, straining towards its stem,
But it was so blue and tall
    That it scorned to think of them!

Red and thirsty were their tongues,
    As the tongues of wolves must be,
But it was so blue and tall—
    Oh, I laughed, I cried, to see!

All my heart became a tear,
    All my soul became a tower,
Never loved I anything
    As I loved that tall blue flower!

It was all the little boats
    That had ever sailed the sea,
It was all the little books
    That had gone to school with me;

On its roots like iron claws
    Rearing up so blue and tall,—
It was all the gallant Earth
    With its back against a wall!

In a breath, ere I had breathed,—
    Oh, I laughed, I cried, to see!—
I was kneeling at its side,
    And it leaned its head on me!

Crumbling stones and sliding sand
    Is the road to Heaven now;
Icy at my straining knees
    Drags the awful under-tow;

Soon but stepping-stones of dust
    Will the road to Heaven be,—
Father, Son and Holy Ghost,
    Reach a hand and rescue me!

"There—there, my blue-flag flower;
    Hush—hush—go to sleep;
That is only God you hear,
    Counting up His folded sheep!

Lullabye—lullabye—
    That is only God that calls,
Missing me, seeking me,
    Ere the road to nothing falls!

He will set His mighty feet
    Firmly on the sliding sand;
Like a little frightened bird
    I will creep into His hand;

I will tell Him all my grief,
    I will tell Him all my sin;
He will give me half His robe
    For a cloak to wrap you in.

Lullabye—lullabye—"
    Rocks the burnt-out planet free!—
Father, Son and Holy Ghost,
    Reach a hand and rescue me!

Ah, the voice of love at last!
    Lo, at last the face of light!
And the whole of His white robe
    For a cloak against the night!

And upon my heart asleep
    All the things I ever knew!—
"Holds Heaven not some cranny, Lord,
    For a flower so tall and blue?"

All's well and all's well!
    Gay the lights of Heaven show!
In some moist and Heavenly place
    We will set it out to grow.

## JOURNEY

Ah, could I lay me down in this long grass
And close my eyes, and let the quiet wind
Blow over me—I am so tired, so tired
Of passing pleasant places! All my life,
Following Care along the dusty road,

Have I looked back at loveliness and sighed;
Yet at my hand an unrelenting hand
Tugged ever, and I passed. All my life long
Over my shoulder have I looked at peace;
And now I fain would lie in this long grass
And close my eyes.
                         Yet onward!
                              Cat birds call
Through the long afternoon, and creeks at dusk
Are guttural. Whip-poor-wills wake and cry,
Drawing the twilight close about their throats.
Only my heart makes answer. Eager vines
Go up the rocks and wait; flushed apple-trees
Pause in their dance and break the ring for me;
Dim, shady wood-roads, redolent of fern
And bayberry, that through sweet bevies thread
Of round-faced roses, pink and petulant,
Look back and beckon ere they disappear.
Only my heart, only my heart responds.
Yet, ah, my path is sweet on either side
All through the dragging day,—sharp underfoot
And hot, and like dead mist the dry dust hangs—
But far, oh, far as passionate eye can reach,
And long, ah, long as rapturous eye can cling,
The world is mine: blue hill, still silver lake,
Broad field, bright flower, and the long white road
A gateless garden, and an open path:
My feet to follow, and my heart to hold.


## EEL-GRASS


No matter what I say,
      All that I really love
Is the rain that flattens on the bay,
      And the eel-grass in the cove;
The jingle-shells that lie and bleach
      At the tide-line, and the trace

Of higher tides along the beach:
   Nothing in this place.

## ELEGY BEFORE DEATH

There will be rose and rhododendron
   When you are dead and under ground;
Still will be heard from white syringas
   Heavy with bees, a sunny sound;

Still will the tamaracks be raining
   After the rain has ceased, and still
Will there be robins in the stubble,
   Brown sheep upon the warm green hill.

Spring will not ail nor autumn falter;
   Nothing will know that you are gone,
Saving alone some sullen plough-land
   None but yourself sets foot upon;

Saving the may-weed and the pig-weed
   Nothing will know that you are dead,—
These, and perhaps a useless wagon
   Standing beside some tumbled shed.

Oh, there will pass with your great passing
   Little of beauty not your own,—
Only the light from common water,
   Only the grace from simple stone!

## THE BEAN-STALK

Ho, Giant! This is I!
I have built me a bean-stalk into your sky!
La,—but it's lovely, up so high!

This is how I came,—I put
Here my knee, there my foot,
Up and up, from shoot to shoot—
And the blessed bean-stalk thinning
Like the mischief all the time,
Till it took me rocking, spinning,
In a dizzy, sunny circle,
Making angles with the root,
Far and out above the cackle
Of the city I was born in,
Till the little dirty city
In the light so sheer and sunny
Shone as dazzling bright and pretty
As the money that you find
In a dream of finding money—
What a wind! What a morning!—

Till the tiny, shiny city,
When I shot a glance below,
Shaken with a giddy laughter,
Sick and blissfully afraid,
Was a dew-drop on a blade,
And a pair of moments after
Was the whirling guess I made,—
And the wind was like a whip

Cracking past my icy ears,
And my hair stood out behind,
And my eyes were full of tears,
Wide-open and cold,
More tears than they could hold,
The wind was blowing so,
And my teeth were in a row,
Dry and grinning,
And I felt my foot slip,
And I scratched the wind and whined,
And I clutched the stalk and jabbered,
With my eyes shut blind,—
What a wind! What a wind!

Your broad sky, Giant,
Is the shelf of a cupboard;
I make bean-stalks, I'm
A builder, like yourself,
But bean-stalks is my trade,
I couldn't make a shelf,
Don't know how they're made,
Now, a bean-stalk is more pliant—
La, what a climb!

# WEEDS

White with daisies and red with sorrel
    And empty, empty under the sky!—
Life is a quest and love a quarrel—
    Here is a place for me to lie.

Daisies spring from damned seeds,
    And this red fire that here I see
Is a worthless crop of crimson weeds,
    Cursed by farmers thriftily.

But here, unhated for an hour,
    The sorrel runs in ragged flame,
The daisy stands, a bastard flower,
    Like flowers that bear an honest name.

And here a while, where no wind brings
    The baying of a pack athirst,
May sleep the sleep of blessed things,
    The blood too bright, the brow accurst.

# PASSER MORTUUS EST

Death devours all lovely things;
    Lesbia with her sparrow

Shares the darkness,—presently
    Every bed is narrow.

Unremembered as old rain
    Dries the sheer libation,
And the little petulant hand
    Is an annotation.

After all, my erstwhile dear,
    My no longer cherished,
Need we say it was not love,
    Now that love is perished?

## PASTORAL

If it were only still!—
With far away the shrill
Crying of a cock;
Or the shaken bell
From a cow's throat
Moving through the bushes;
Or the soft shock
Of wizened apples falling
From an old tree
In a forgotten orchard
Upon the hilly rock!

Oh, grey hill,
Where the grazing herd
Licks the purple blossom,
Crops the spiky weed!
Oh, stony pasture,
Where the tall mullein
Stands up so sturdy
On its little seed!

# ASSAULT

## I

I had forgotten how the frogs must sound
After a year of silence, else I think
I should not so have ventured forth alone
At dusk upon this unfrequented road.

## II

I am waylaid by Beauty. Who will walk
Between me and the crying of the frogs?
Oh, savage Beauty, suffer me to pass,
That am a timid woman, on her way
From one house to another!

# TRAVEL

The railroad track is miles away,
 And the day is loud with voices speaking,
Yet there isn't a train goes by all day
 But I hear its whistle shrieking.

All night there isn't a train goes by,
 Though the night is still for sleep and dreaming
But I see its cinders red on the sky,
 And hear its engine steaming.

My heart is warm with the friends I make,
 And better friends I'll not be knowing,
Yet there isn't a train I wouldn't take,
 No matter where it's going.

# LOW-TIDE

These wet rocks where the tide has been,
    Barnacled white and weeded brown
And slimed beneath to a beautiful green,
    These wet rocks where the tide went down
Will show again when the tide is high
    Faint and perilous, far from shore,
No place to dream, but a place to die,—
    The bottom of the sea once more.
There was a child that wandered through
    A giant's empty house all day,—
House full of wonderful things and new,
    But no fit place for a child to play.

# SONG OF A SECOND APRIL

*Pain of bereavement*

April this year, not otherwise
    Than April of a year ago,
Is full of whispers, full of sighs,
    Of dazzling mud and dingy snow;
    Hepaticas that pleased you so
Are here again, and butterflies.

There rings a hammering all day,
    And shingles lie about the doors;
In orchards near and far away
    The grey wood-pecker taps and bores;
    The men are merry at their chores,
And children earnest at their play.

The larger streams run still and deep,
    Noisy and swift the small brooks run
Among the mullein stalks the sheep
    Go up the hillside in the sun,
    Pensively,—only you are gone,
You that alone I cared to keep.

# ROSEMARY

For the sake of some things
    That be now no more
I will strew rushes
    On my chamber-floor,
I will plant bergamot
    At my kitchen-door.

For the sake of dim things
    That were once so plain
I will set a barrel
    Out to catch the rain,
I will hang an iron pot
    On an iron crane.

Many things be dead and gone
    That were brave and gay;
For the sake of these things
    I will learn to say,
"An it please you, gentle sirs,"
    "Alack!" and "Well-a-day!"

# THE POET AND HIS BOOK

Down, you mongrel, Death!
    Back into your kennel!
I have stolen breath
    In a stalk of fennel!
You shall scratch and you shall whine
    Many a night, and you shall worry
    Many a bone, before you bury
One sweet bone of mine!

When shall I be dead?
    When my flesh is withered,
And above my head

Yellow pollen gathered
All the empty afternoon?
    When sweet lovers pause and wonder
    Who am I that lie thereunder,
Hidden from the moon?

This my personal death?—
    That lungs be failing
To inhale the breath
    Others are exhaling?
This my subtle spirit's end?—
    Ah, when the thawed winter splashes
    Over these chance dust and ashes,
Weep not me, my friend!

Me, by no means dead
    In that hour, but surely
When this book, unread,
    Rots to earth obscurely,
And no more to any breast,
    Close against the clamorous swelling
    Of the thing there is no telling,
Are these pages pressed!

When this book is mould,
    And a book of many
Waiting to be sold
    For a casual penny,
In a little open case,
    In a street unclean and cluttered,
    Where a heavy mud is spattered
From the passing drays,

Stranger, pause and look;
    From the dust of ages
Lift this little book,
    Turn the tattered pages,
Read me, do not let me die!
    Search the fading letters, finding

Steadfast in the broken binding
All that once was I!

When these veins are weeds,
　　When these hollowed sockets
Watch the rooty seeds
　　Bursting down like rockets,
And surmise the spring again,
　　Or, remote in that black cupboard,
　　Watch the pink worms writhing upward
At the smell of rain,

Boys and girls that lie
　　Whispering in the hedges,
Do not let me die,
　　Mix me with your pledges;
Boys and girls that slowly walk
　　In the woods, and weep, and quarrel,
　　Staring past the pink wild laurel,
Mix me with your talk,

Do not let me die!
　　Farmers at your raking,
When the sun is high,
　　While the hay is making,
When, along the stubble strewn,
　　Withering on their stalks uneaten,
　　Strawberries turn dark and sweeten
In the lapse of noon;

Shepherds on the hills,
　　In the pastures, drowsing
To the tinkling bells
　　Of the brown sheep browsing;
Sailors crying through the storm;
　　Scholars at your study; hunters
　　Lost amid the whirling winter's
Whiteness uniform;

Men that long for sleep;
　　Men that wake and revel;—
If an old song leap
　　To your senses' level
At such moments, may it be
　　Sometimes, though a moment only,
　　Some forgotten, quaint and homely
Vehicle of me!

Women at your toil,
　　Women at your leisure
Till the kettle boil,
　　Snatch of me your pleasure,
Where the broom-straw marks the leaf;
　　Women quiet with your weeping
　　Lest you wake a workman sleeping,
Mix me with your grief!

Boys and girls that steal
　　From the shocking laughter
Of the old, to kneel
　　By a dripping rafter
Under the discolored eaves,
　　Out of trunks with hingeless covers
　　Lifting tales of saints and lovers,
Travelers, goblins, thieves,

Suns that shine by night,
　　Mountains made from valleys,—
Bear me to the light,
　　Flat upon your bellies
By the webby window lie,
　　Where the little flies are crawling,—
　　Read me, margin me with scrawling,
Do not let me die!

Sexton, ply your trade!
　　In a shower of gravel
Stamp upon your spade!

Many a rose shall ravel,
Many a metal wreath shall rust
    In the rain, and I go singing
    Through the lots where you are flinging
Yellow clay on dust!

## ALMS

*a woman feels
she is no
longer loved.
and depression
descends on her*

My heart is what it was before,
    A house where people come and go;
But it is winter with your love,
    The sashes are beset with snow.

I light the lamp and lay the cloth,
    I blow the coals to blaze again;
But it is winter with your love,
    The frost is thick upon the pane.

I know a winter when it comes:
    The leaves are listless on the boughs;
I watched your love a little while,
    And brought my plants into the house.

I water them and turn them south,
    I snap the dead brown from the stem;
But it is winter with your love,—
    I only tend and water them.

There was a time I stood and watched
    The small, ill-natured sparrows' fray;
I loved the beggar that I fed,
    I cared for what he had to say,

I stood and watched him out of sight;
    Today I reach around the door
And set a bowl upon the step;
    My heart is what it was before,

But it is winter with your love;
    I scatter crumbs upon the sill,
And close the window,—and the birds
    May take or leave them, as they will.

## INLAND

People that build their houses inland,
    People that buy a plot of ground
Shaped like a house, and build a house there,
    Far from the sea-board, far from the sound

Of water sucking the hollow ledges,
    Tons of water striking the shore,—
What do they long for, as I long for
    One salt smell of the sea once more?

People the waves have not awakened,
    Spanking the boats at the harbor's head,
What do they long for, as I long for,—
    Starting up in my inland bed,

Beating the narrow walls, and finding
    Neither a window nor a door,
Screaming to God for death by drowning,—
    One salt taste of the sea once more?

## TO A POET THAT DIED YOUNG

Minstrel, what have you to do
With this man that, after you,
Sharing not your happy fate,
Sat as England's Laureate?
Vainly, in these iron days,
Strives the poet in your praise,
Minstrel, by whose singing side
Beauty walked, until you died.

Still, though none should hark again,
Drones the blue-fly in the pane,
Thickly crusts the blackest moss,
Blows the rose its musk across,
Floats the boat that is forgot
None the less to Camelot.

Many a bard's untimely death
Lends unto his verses breath;
Here's a song was never sung:
Growing old is dying young.
Minstrel, what is this to you:
That a man you never knew,
When your grave was far and green,
Sat and gossipped with a queen?

Thalia knows how rare a thing
Is it, to grow old and sing;
When a brown and tepid tide
Closes in on every side.
Who shall say if Shelley's gold
Had withstood it to grow old?

# WRAITH

"Thin Rain, whom are you haunting,
    That you haunt my door?"
—Surely it is not I she's wanting;
    Someone living here before—
"Nobody's in the house but me:
You may come in if you like and see."

Thin as thread, with exquisite fingers,—
    Have you seen her, any of you?—
Grey shawl, and leaning on the wind,
    And the garden showing through?

Glimmering eyes,—and silent, mostly,
Sort of a whisper, sort of a purr,
Asking something, asking it over,
If you get a sound from her.—

Ever see her, any of you?—
Strangest thing I've ever known,—
Every night since I moved in,
And I came to be alone.

"Thin Rain, hush with your knocking!
You may not come in!
This is I that you hear rocking;
Nobody's with me, nor has been!"

Curious, how she tried the window,—
Odd, the way she tries the door,—
Wonder just what sort of people
Could have had this house before . . .

## EBB

I know what my heart is like
Since your love died:
It is like a hollow ledge
Holding a little pool
Left there by the tide,
A little tepid pool,
Drying inward from the edge.

## ELAINE

OH, come again to Astolat!
I will not ask you to be kind.
And you may go when you will go,
And I will stay behind.

I will not say how dear you are,
  Or ask you if you hold me dear,
Or trouble you with things for you
  The way I did last year.

So still the orchard, Lancelot,
  So very still the lake shall be,
You could not guess—though you should guess—
  What is become of me.

So wide shall be the garden-walk,
  The garden-seat so very wide,
You needs must think—if you should think—
  The lily maid had died.

Save that, a little way away,
  I'd watch you for a little while,
To see you speak, the way you speak,
  And smile,—if you should smile.

# BURIAL

Mine is a body that should die at sea!
  And have for a grave, instead of a grave
Six feet deep and the length of me,
  All the water that is under the wave!

And terrible fishes to seize my flesh,
  Such as a living man might fear,
And eat me while I am firm and fresh,—
  Not wait till I've been dead for a year!

# MARIPOSA

Butterflies are white and blue
In this field we wander through.

Suffer me to take your hand.
Death comes in a day or two.

All the things we ever knew
Will be ashes in that hour,
Mark the transient butterfly,
How he hangs upon the flower.

Suffer me to take your hand.
Suffer me to cherish you
Till the dawn is in the sky.
Whether I be false or true,
Death comes in a day or two.

## THE LITTLE HILL

OH, here the air is sweet and still,
    And soft's the grass to lie on;
And far away's the little hill
    They took for Christ to die on.

And there's a hill across the brook,
    And down the brook's another;
But, oh, the little hill they took,—
    I think I am its mother!

The moon that saw Gethsemane,
    I watch it rise and set:
It has so many things to see,
    They help it to forget.

But little hills that sit at home
    So many hundred years,
Remember Greece, remember Rome,
    Remember Mary's tears.

And far away in Palestine,
    Sadder than any other,
Grieves still the hill that I call mine,—
    I think I am its mother!

# DOUBT NO MORE THAT OBERON

Doubt no more that Oberon—
Never doubt that Pan
Lived, and played a reed, and ran
After nymphs in a dark forest,
In the merry, credulous days,—
Lived, and led a fairy band
Over the indulgent land!
Ah, for in this dourest, sorest
Age man's eye has looked upon,
Death to fauns and death to fays,
Still the dog-wood dares to raise—
Healthy tree, with trunk and root—
Ivory bowls that bear no fruit,
And the starlings and the jays—
Birds that cannot even sing—
Dare to come again in spring!

# LAMENT

Listen, children:
Your father is dead.
From his old coats
I'll make you little jackets;
I'll make you little trousers
From his old pants.
There'll be in his pockets
Things he used to put there,
Keys and pennies
Covered with tobacco;

Dan shall have the pennies
To save in his bank;
Anne shall have the keys
To make a pretty noise with.
Life must go on,
And the dead be forgotten;
Life must go on,
Though good men die;
Anne, eat your breakfast;
Dan, take your medicine;
Life must go on;
I forget just why.

## EXILED

Searching my heart for its true sorrow,
    This is the thing I find to be:
That I am weary of words and people,
    Sick of the city, wanting the sea;

Wanting the sticky, salty sweetness
    Of the strong wind and shattered spray;
Wanting the loud sound and the soft sound
    Of the big surf that breaks all day.

Always before about my dooryard,
    Marking the reach of the winter sea,
Rooted in sand and dragging drift-wood,
    Straggled the purple wild sweet-pea;

Always I climbed the wave at morning,
    Shook the sand from my shoes at night,
That now am caught beneath great buildings,
    Stricken with noise, confused with light.

If I could hear the green piles groaning
    Under the windy wooden piers,

See once again the bobbing barrels,
    And the black sticks that fence the weirs,

If I could see the weedy mussels
    Crusting the wrecked and rotting hulls,
Hear once again the hungry crying
    Overhead, of the wheeling gulls,

Feel once again the shanty straining
    Under the turning of the tide,
Fear once again the rising freshet,
    Dread the bell in the fog outside,—

I should be happy,—that was happy
    All day long on the coast of Maine!
I have a need to hold and handle
    Shells and anchors and ships again!

I should be happy, that am happy
    Never at all since I came here.
I am too long away from water.
    I have a need of water near.

## THE DEATH OF AUTUMN

When reeds are dead and a straw to thatch the marshes,
And feathered pampas-grass rides into the wind
Like aged warriors westward, tragic, thinned
Of half their tribe, and over the flattened rushes,
Stripped of its secret, open, stark and bleak,
Blackens afar the half-forgotten creek,—
Then leans on me the weight of the year, and crushes
My heart. I know that Beauty must ail and die,
And will be born again,—but ah, to see
Beauty stiffened, staring up at the sky!
Oh, Autumn! Autumn!—What is the Spring to me?

# ODE TO SILENCE

Aye, but she?
Your other sister and my other soul
Grave Silence, lovelier
Than the three loveliest maidens, what of her?
Clio, not you,
Not you, Calliope,
Nor all your wanton line,
Not Beauty's perfect self shall comfort me
For Silence once departed,
For her the cool-tongued, her the tranquil-hearted,
Whom evermore I follow wistfully,
Wandering Heaven and Earth and Hell and the four seasons through;
Thalia, not you,
Not you, Melpomene,
Not your incomparable feet, O thin Terpsichore,
I seek in this great hall,
But one more pale, more pensive, most beloved of you all.
I seek her from afar,
I come from temples where her altars are,
From groves that bear her name,
Noisy with stricken victims now and sacrificial flame,
And cymbals struck on high and strident faces
Obstreperous in her praise
They neither love nor know,
A goddess of gone days,
Departed long ago,
Abandoning the invaded shrines and fanes
Of her old sanctuary,
A deity obscure and legendary,
Of whom there now remains,
For sages to decipher and priests to garble,
Only and for a little while her letters wedged in marble,
Which even now, behold, the friendly mumbling rain erases,
And the inarticulate snow,
Leaving at last of her least signs and traces
None whatsoever, nor whither she is vanished from these places.

"She will love well," I said,
"If love be of that heart inhabiter,
The flowers of the dead;
The red anemone that with no sound
Moves in the wind, and from another wound
That sprang, the heavily-sweet blue hyacinth,
That blossoms underground,
And sallow poppies, will be dear to her.
And will not Silence know
In the black shade of what obsidian steep
Stiffens the white narcissus numb with sleep?
(Seed which Demeter's daughter bore from home,
Uptorn by desperate fingers long ago,
Reluctant even as she,
Undone Persephone,
And even as she set out again to grow
In twilight, in perdition's lean and inauspicious loam).
She will love well," I said,
"The flowers of the dead;
Where dark Persephone the winter round,
Uncomforted for home, uncomforted,
Lacking a sunny southern slope in northern Sicily,
With sullen pupils focussed on a dream,
Stares on the stagnant stream
That moats the unequivocable battlements of Hell,
There, there will she be found,
She that is Beauty veiled from men and Music in a swound."

"I long for Silence as they long for breath
Whose helpless nostrils drink the bitter sea;
What thing can be
So stout, what so redoubtable, in Death
What fury, what considerable rage, if only she,
Upon whose icy breast,
Unquestioned, uncaressed,
One time I lay,
And whom always I lack,
Even to this day,
Being by no means from that frigid bosom weaned away,

If only she therewith be given me back?"
I sought her down that dolorous labyrinth,
Wherein no shaft of sunlight ever fell,
And in among the bloodless everywhere
I sought her, but the air,
Breathed many times and spent,
Was fretful with a whispering discontent,
And questioning me, importuning me to tell
Some slightest tidings of the light of day they know no more,
Plucking my sleeve, the eager shades were with me where I went.
I paused at every grievous door,
And harked a moment, holding up my hand,—and for a space
A hush was on them, while they watched my face;
And then they fell a-whispering as before;
So that I smiled at them and left them, seeing she was not there.
I sought her, too,
Among the upper gods, although I knew
She was not like to be where feasting is,
Nor near to Heaven's lord,
Being a thing abhorred
And shunned of him, although a child of his,
(Not yours, not yours; to you she owes not breath,
Mother of Song, being sown of Zeus upon a dream of Death).
Fearing to pass unvisited some place
And later learn, too late, how all the while,
With her still face,
She had been standing there and seen me pass, without a smile,
I sought her even to the sagging board whereat
The stout immortals sat;
But such a laughter shook the mighty hall
No one could hear me say:
Had she been seen upon the Hill that day?
And no one knew at all
How long I stood, or when at last I sighed and went away.

There is a garden lying in a lull
Between the mountains and the mountainous sea,
I know not where, but which a dream diurnal
Paints on my lids a moment till the hull

Be lifted from the kernel
And Slumber fed to me.
Your foot-print is not there, Mnemosene,
Though it would seem a ruined place and after
Your lichenous heart, being full
Of broken columns, caryatides
Thrown to the earth and fallen forward on their jointless knees,
And urns funereal altered into dust
Minuter than the ashes of the dead,
And Psyche's lamp out of the earth up-thrust,
Dripping itself in marble wax on what was once the bed
Of Love, and his young body asleep, but now is dust instead.

There twists the bitter-sweet, the white wisteria
Fastens its fingers in the strangling wall,
And the wide crannies quicken with bright weeds;
There dumbly like a worm all day the still white orchid feeds;
But never an echo of your daughters' laughter
Is there, nor any sign of you at all
Swells fungous from the rotten bough, grey mother of Pieria!

Only her shadow once upon a stone
I saw,—and, lo, the shadow and the garden, too, were gone.

I tell you you have done her body an ill,
You chatterers, you noisy crew!
She is not anywhere!
I sought her in deep Hell;
And through the world as well;
I thought of Heaven and I sought her there;
Above nor under ground
Is Silence to be found,
That was the very warp and woof of you,
Lovely before your songs began and after they were through!
Oh, say if on this hill
Somewhere your sister's body lies in death,
So I may follow there, and make a wreath
Of my locked hands, that on her quiet breast
Shall lie till age has withered them!

(Ah, sweetly from the rest
I see
Turn and consider me
Compassionate Euterpe!)
"There is a gate beyond the gate of Death,
Beyond the gate of everlasting Life,
Beyond the gates of Heaven and Hell," she saith,
"Whereon but to believe is horror!
Whereon to meditate engendereth
Even in deathless spirits such as I
A tumult in the breath,
A chilling of the inexhaustible blood
Even in my veins that never will be dry,
And in the austere, divine monotony
That is my being, the madness of an unaccustomed mood.

This is her province whom you lack and seek;
And seek her not elsewhere.
Hell is a thoroughfare
For pilgrims,—Herakles,
And he that loved Euridice too well,
Have walked therein; and many more than these;
And witnessed the desire and the despair
Of souls that passed reluctantly and sicken for the air;
You, too, have entered Hell,
And issued thence; but thence whereof I speak
None has returned;—for thither fury brings
Only the driven ghosts of them that flee before all things.
Oblivion is the name of this abode: and she is there."

Oh, radiant Song! Oh, gracious Memory!
Be long upon this height
I shall not climb again!
I know the way you mean,—the little night,
And the long empty day,—never to see
Again the angry light,
Or hear the hungry noises cry my brain!
Ah, but she,
Your other sister and my other soul,

She shall again be mine;
And I shall drink her from a silver bowl,
A chilly thin green wine,
Not bitter to the taste,
Not sweet,
Not of your press, oh, restless, clamorous nine,—
To foam beneath the frantic hoofs of mirth—
But savoring faintly of the acid earth,
And trod by pensive feet
From perfect clusters ripened without haste
Out of the urgent heat
In some clear glimmering vaulted twilight under the odorous vine.

Lift up your lyres! Sing on!
But as for me, I seek your sister whither she is gone.

# MEMORIAL TO D. C.
## [VASSAR COLLEGE, 1918]

Oh, loveliest throat of all sweet throats,
    Where now no more the music is,
With hands that wrote you little notes
    I write you little elegies!

# EPITAPH

Heap not on this mound
    Roses that she loved so well;
Why bewilder her with roses,
    That she cannot see or smell?
She is happy where she lies
    With the dust upon her eyes.

# PRAYER TO PERSEPHONE

Be to her, Persephone,
All the things I might not be;
Take her head upon your knee.
She that was so proud and wild,
Flippant, arrogant and free,
She that had no need of me,
Is a little lonely child
Lost in Hell,—Persephone,
Take her head upon your knee;
Say to her, "My dear, my dear,
It is not so dreadful here."

# CHORUS

Give away her gowns,
Give away her shoes;
She has no more use
For her fragrant gowns;
Take them all down,
Blue, green, blue,
Lilac, pink, blue,
From their padded hangers;
She will dance no more
In her narrow shoes;
Sweep her narrow shoes
From the closet floor.

# ELEGY

Let them bury your big eyes
In the secret earth securely,
Your thin fingers, and your fair,
Soft, indefinite-colored hair,—
All of these in some way, surely,

From the secret earth shall rise;
Not for these I sit and stare,
Broken and bereft completely;
Your young flesh that sat so neatly
On your little bones will sweetly
Blossom in the air.

But your voice,—never the rushing
Of a river underground,
Not the rising of the wind
In the trees before the rain,
Not the woodcock's watery call,
Not the note the white-throat utters,
Not the feet of children pushing
Yellow leaves along the gutters
In the blue and bitter fall,
Shall content my musing mind
For the beauty of that sound
That in no new way at all
Ever will be heard again.

Sweetly through the sappy stalk
Of the vigorous weed,
Holding all it held before,
Cherished by the faithful sun,
On and on eternally
Shall your altered fluid run,
Bud and bloom and go to seed;
But your singing days are done;
But the music of your talk
Never shall the chemistry
Of the secret earth restore.
All your lovely words are spoken.
Once the ivory box is broken,
Beats the golden bird no more.

# DIRGE

Boys and girls that held her dear,
    Do your weeping now;
All you loved of her lies here.

Brought to earth the arrogant brow,
    And the withering tongue
Chastened; do your weeping now.

Sing whatever songs are sung,
    Wind whatever wreath,
For a playmate perished young,

For a spirit spent in death.
Boys and girls that held her dear,
All you loved of her lies here.

# SONNETS

## I

We talk of taxes, and I call you friend;
Well, such you are,—but well enough we know
How thick about us root, how rankly grow
Those subtle weeds no man has need to tend,
That flourish through neglect, and soon must send
Perfume too sweet upon us and overthrow
Our steady senses; how such matters go
We are aware, and how such matters end.
Yet shall be told no meagre passion here;
With lovers such as we forevermore
Isolde drinks the draught, and Guinevere
Receives the Table's ruin through her door,
Francesca, with the loud surf at her ear,
Lets fall the colored book upon the floor.

## II

Into the golden vessel of great song
Let us pour all our passion; breast to breast
Let other lovers lie, in love and rest;
Not we,—articulate, so, but with the tongue
Of all the world: the churning blood, the long
Shuddering quiet, the desperate hot palms pressed
Sharply together upon the escaping guest,
The common soul, unguarded, and grown strong.
Longing alone is singer to the lute;
Let still on nettles in the open sigh
The minstrel, that in slumber is as mute
As any man, and love be far and high,
That else forsakes the topmost branch, a fruit
Found on the ground by every passer-by.

## III

Not with libations, but with shouts and laughter
We drenched the altars of Love's sacred grove,
Shaking to earth green fruits, impatient after
The launching of the colored moths of Love.
Love's proper myrtle and his mother's zone
We bound about our irreligious brows,
And fettered him with garlands of our own,
And spread a banquet in his frugal house.
Not yet the god has spoken; but I fear
Though we should break our bodies in his flame,
And pour our blood upon his altar, here
Henceforward is a grove without a name,
A pasture to the shaggy goats of Pan,
Whence flee forever a woman and a man.

## IV

Only until this cigarette is ended,
A little moment at the end of all,
While on the floor the quiet ashes fall,

And in the firelight to a lance extended,
Bizarrely with the jazzing music blended,
The broken shadow dances on the wall,
I will permit my memory to recall
The vision of you, by all my dreams attended.
And then adieu,—farewell!—the dream is done.
Yours is a face of which I can forget
The color and the features, every one,
The words not ever, and the smiles not yet;
But in your day this moment is the sun
Upon a hill, after the sun has set.

V

Once more into my arid days like dew,
Like wind from an oasis, or the sound
Of cold sweet water bubbling underground,
A treacherous messenger, the thought of you
Comes to destroy me; once more I renew
Firm faith in your abundance, whom I found
Long since to be but just one other mound
Of sand, whereon no green thing ever grew.
And once again, and wiser in no wise,
I chase your colored phantom on the air,
And sob and curse and fall and weep and rise
And stumble pitifully on to where,
Miserable and lost, with stinging eyes,
Once more I clasp,—and there is nothing there.

VI

No rose that in a garden ever grew,
In Homer's or in Omar's or in mine,
Though buried under centuries of fine
Dead dust of roses, shut from sun and dew
Forever, and forever lost from view,
But must again in fragrance rich as wine
The grey aisles of the air incarnadine
When the old summers surge into a new.

Thus when I swear, "I love with all my heart,"
'Tis with the heart of Lilith that I swear,
'Tis with the love of Lesbia and Lucrece;
And thus as well my love must lose some part
Of what it is, had Helen been less fair,
Or perished young, or stayed at home in Greece.


## VII

When I too long have looked upon your face,
Wherein for me a brightness unobscured
Save by the mists of brightness has its place,
And terrible beauty not to be endured,
I turn away reluctant from your light,
And stand irresolute, a mind undone,
A silly, dazzled thing deprived of sight
From having looked too long upon the sun.
Then is my daily life a narrow room
In which a little while, uncertainly,
Surrounded by impenetrable gloom,
Among familiar things grown strange to me
Making my way, I pause, and feel, and hark,
Till I become accustomed to the dark.


## VIII

And you as well must die, beloved dust,
And all your beauty stand you in no stead;
This flawless, vital hand, this perfect head,
This body of flame and steel, before the gust
Of Death, or under his autumnal frost,
Shall be as any leaf, be no less dead
Than the first leaf that fell,—this wonder fled.
Altered, estranged, disintegrated, lost.
Nor shall my love avail you in your hour.
In spite of all my love, you will arise
Upon that day and wander down the air
Obscurely as the unattended flower,
It mattering not how beautiful you were,
Or how beloved above all else that dies.

## IX

Let you not say of me when I am old,
In pretty worship of my withered hands
Forgetting who I am, and how the sands
Of such a life as mine run red and gold
Even to the ultimate sifting dust, "Behold,
Here walketh passionless age!"—for there expands
A curious superstition in these lands,
And by its leave some weightless tales are told.

In me no lenten wicks watch out the night;
I am the booth where Folly holds her fair;
Impious no less in ruin than in strength,
When I lie crumbled to the earth at length,
Let you not say, "Upon this reverend site
The righteous groaned and beat their breasts in prayer."

## X

Oh, my beloved, have you thought of this:
How in the years to come unscrupulous Time,
More cruel than Death, will tear you from my kiss,
And make you old, and leave me in my prime?
How you and I, who scale together yet
A little while the sweet, immortal height
No pilgrim may remember or forget,
As sure as the world turns, some granite night
Shall lie awake and know the gracious flame
Gone out forever on the mutual stone;
And call to mind that on the day you came
I was a child, and you a hero grown?—
And the night pass, and the strange morning break
Upon our anguish for each other's sake!

## XI

As to some lovely temple, tenantless
Long since, that once was sweet with shivering brass,
Knowing well its altars ruined and the grass

Grown up between the stones, yet from excess
Of grief hard driven, or great loneliness,
The worshiper returns, and those who pass
Marvel him crying on a name that was,—
So is it now with me in my distress.
Your body was a temple to Delight;
Cold are its ashes whence the breath is fled,
Yet here one time your spirit was wont to move;
Here might I hope to find you day or night,
And here I come to look for you, my love,
Even now, foolishly, knowing you are dead.

### XII

Cherish you then the hope I shall forget
At length, my lord, Pieria?—put away
For your so passing sake, this mouth of clay
These mortal bones against my body set,
For all the puny fever and frail sweat
Of human love,—renounce for these, I say,
The Singing Mountain's memory, and betray
The silent lyre that hangs upon me yet?
Ah, but indeed, some day shall you awake,
Rather, from dreams of me, that at your side
So many nights, a lover and a bride,
But stern in my soul's chastity, have lain,
To walk the world forever for my sake,
And in each chamber find me gone again!

## WILD SWANS

I looked in my heart while the wild swans went over.
And what did I see I had not seen before?
Only a question less or a question more;
Nothing to match the flight of wild birds flying.
Tiresome heart, forever living and dying,
House without air, I leave you and lock your door.
Wild swans, come over the town, come over
The town again, trailing your legs and crying!

# RENASCENCE AND OTHER POEMS

# RENASCENCE

All I could see from where I stood
Was three long mountains and a wood;
I turned and looked another way,
And saw three islands in a bay.
So with my eyes I traced the line
Of the horizon, thin and fine,
Straight around till I was come
Back to where I'd started from;
And all I saw from where I stood
Was three long mountains and a wood.
Over these things I could not see;
These were the things that bounded me;
And I could touch them with my hand,
Almost, I thought, from where I stand.
And all at once things seemed so small
My breath came short, and scarce at all.
But, sure, the sky is big, I said;
Miles and miles above my head;
So here upon my back I'll lie
And look my fill into the sky.
And so I looked, and, after all,
The sky was not so very tall.
The sky, I said, must somewhere stop,
And—sure enough!—I see the top!
The sky, I thought, is not so grand;
I 'most could touch it with my hand!
And reaching up my hand to try,
I screamed to feel it touch the sky.
I screamed, and—lo!—Infinity
Came down and settled over me;

Forced back my scream into my chest,
Bent back my arm upon my breast,
And, pressing of the Undefined
The definition on my mind,
Held up before my eyes a glass
Through which my shrinking sight did pass
Until it seemed I must behold
Immensity made manifold;
Whispered to me a word whose sound
Deafened the air for worlds around,
And brought unmuffled to my ears
The gossiping of friendly spheres,
The creaking of the tented sky,
The ticking of Eternity.
I saw and heard, and knew at last
The How and Why of all things, past,
And present, and forevermore.
The Universe, cleft to the core,
Lay open to my probing sense
That, sick'ning, I would fain pluck thence
But could not,—nay! But needs must suck
At the great wound, and could not pluck
My lips away till I had drawn
All venom out.—Ah, fearful pawn!
For my omniscience paid I toll
In infinite remorse of soul.
All sin was of my sinning, all
Atoning mine, and mine the gall
Of all regret. Mine was the weight
Of every brooded wrong, the hate
That stood behind each envious thrust,
Mine every greed, mine every lust.
And all the while for every grief,
Each suffering, I craved relief
With individual desire,—
Craved all in vain! And felt fierce fire
About a thousand people crawl;
Perished with each,—then mourned for all!
A man was starving in Capri;

He moved his eyes and looked at me;
I felt his gaze, I heard his moan,
And knew his hunger as my own.
I saw at sea a great fog bank
Between two ships that struck and sank;
A thousand screams the heavens smote;
And every scream tore through my throat.
No hurt I did not feel, no death
That was not mine; mine each last breath
That, crying, met an answering cry
From the compassion that was I.
All suffering mine, and mine its rod;
Mine, pity like the pity of God.
Ah, awful weight! Infinity
Pressed down upon the finite Me!
My anguished spirit, like a bird,
Beating against my lips I heard;
Yet lay the weight so close about
There was no room for it without.
And so beneath the weight lay I
And suffered death, but could not die.

Long had I lain thus, craving death,
When quietly the earth beneath
Gave way, and inch by inch, so great
At last had grown the crushing weight,
Into the earth I sank till I
Full six feet under ground did lie,
And sank no more,—there is no weight
Can follow here, however great.
From off my breast I felt it roll,
And as it went my tortured soul
Burst forth and fled in such a gust
That all about me swirled the dust.

Deep in the earth I rested now;
Cool is its hand upon the brow
And soft its breast beneath the head
Of one who is so gladly dead.

And all at once, and over all
The pitying rain began to fall;
I lay and heard each pattering hoof
Upon my lowly, thatched roof,
And seemed to love the sound far more
Than ever I had done before.
For rain it hath a friendly sound
To one who's six feet underground;
And scarce the friendly voice or face:
A grave is such a quiet place.

The rain, I said, is kind to come
And speak to me in my new home.
I would I were alive again
To kiss the fingers of the rain,
To drink into my eyes the shine
Of every slanting silver line,
To catch the freshened, fragrant breeze
From drenched and dripping apple-trees.
For soon the shower will be done,
And then the broad face of the sun
Will laugh above the rain-soaked earth
Until the world with answering mirth
Shakes joyously, and each round drop
Rolls, twinkling, from its grass-blade top.
How can I bear it; buried here,
While overhead the sky grows clear
And blue again after the storm?
O, multi-colored, multiform,
Beloved beauty over me,
That I shall never, never see
Again! Spring-silver, autumn-gold,
That I shall never more behold!
Sleeping your myriad magics through,
Close-sepulchred away from you!
O God, I cried, give me new birth,
And put me back upon the earth!
Upset each cloud's gigantic gourd
And let the heavy rain, down-poured

In one big torrent, set me free,
Washing my grave away from me!

I ceased; and through the breathless hush
That answered me, the far-off rush
Of herald wings came whispering
Like music down the vibrant string
Of my ascending prayer, and—crash!
Before the wild wind's whistling lash
The startled storm-clouds reared on high
And plunged in terror down the sky,
And the big rain in one black wave
Fell from the sky and struck my grave.
I know not how such things can be;
I only know there came to me
A fragrance such as never clings
To aught save happy living things;
A sound as of some joyous elf
Singing sweet songs to please himself,
And, through and over everything,
A sense of glad awakening.
The grass, a-tiptoe at my ear,
Whispering to me I could hear;
I felt the rain's cool finger-tips
Brushed tenderly across my lips,
Laid gently on my sealed sight,
And all at once the heavy night
Fell from my eyes and I could see,—
A drenched and dripping apple-tree,
A last long line of silver rain,
A sky grown clear and blue again.
And as I looked a quickening gust
Of wind blew up to me and thrust
Into my face a miracle
Of orchard-breath, and with the smell,—
I know not how such things can be!—
I breathed my soul back into me.
Ah! Up then from the ground sprang I
And hailed the earth with such a cry

As is not heard save from a man
Who has been dead, and lives again.
About the trees my arms I wound;
Like one gone mad I hugged the ground;
I raised my quivering arms on high;
I laughed and laughed into the sky,
Till at my throat a strangling sob
Caught fiercely, and a great heart-throb
Sent instant tears into my eyes;
O God, I cried, no dark disguise
Can e'er hereafter hide from me
Thy radiant identity!
Thou canst not move across the grass
But my quick eyes will see Thee pass,
Nor speak, however silently,
But my hushed voice will answer Thee.
I know the path that tells Thy way
Through the cool eve of every day;
God, I can push the grass apart
And lay my finger on Thy heart!

The world stands out on either side
No wider than the heart is wide;
Above the world is stretched the sky,—
No higher than the soul is high.
The heart can push the sea and land
Farther away on either hand;
The soul can split the sky in two,
And let the face of God shine through.
But East and West will pinch the heart
That can not keep them pushed apart;
And he whose soul is flat—the sky
Will cave in on him by and by.

# Interim

The room is full of you!—As I came in
And closed the door behind me, all at once
A something in the air, intangible,
Yet stiff with meaning, struck my senses sick!—

Sharp, unfamiliar odors have destroyed
Each other room's dear personality.
The heavy scent of damp, funereal flowers,—
The very essence, hush-distilled, of Death—
Has strangled that habitual breath of home
Whose expiration leaves all houses dead;
And wheresoe'er I look is hideous change.
Save here. Here 'twas as if a weed-choked gate
Had opened at my touch, and I had stepped
Into some long-forgot, enchanted, strange,
Sweet garden of a thousand years ago
And suddenly thought, "I have been here before!"

You are not here. I know that you are gone,
And will not ever enter here again.
And yet it seems to me, if I should speak,
Your silent step must wake across the hall;
If I should turn my head, that your sweet eyes
Would kiss me from the door.—So short a time
To teach my life its transposition to
This difficult and unaccustomed key!—
The room is as you left it; your last touch—
A thoughtless pressure, knowing not itself
As saintly—hallows now each simple thing;
Hallows and glorifies, and glows between
The dust's grey fingers like a shielded light.

There is your book, just as you laid it down,
Face to the table,—I cannot believe
That you are gone!—Just then it seemed to me
You must be here. I almost laughed to think

How like reality the dream had been;
Yet knew before I laughed, and so was still.
That book, outspread, just as you laid it down!
Perhaps you thought, "I wonder what comes next,
And whether this or this will be the end";
So rose, and left it, thinking to return.

Perhaps that chair, when you arose and passed
Out of the room, rocked silently a while
Ere it again was still. When you were gone
Forever from the room, perhaps that chair,
Stirred by your movement, rocked a little while,
Silently, to and fro. . .

And here are the last words your fingers wrote,
Scrawled in broad characters across a page
In this brown book I gave you. Here your hand,
Guiding your rapid pen, moved up and down.
Here with a looping knot you crossed a "t",
And here another like it, just beyond
These two eccentric "e's". You were so small,
And wrote so brave a hand!
                              How strange it seems
That of all words these are the words you chose!
And yet a simple choice; you did not know
You would not write again. If you had known—
But then, it does not matter,—and indeed
If you had known there was so little time
You would have dropped your pen and come to me
And this page would be empty, and some phrase
Other than this would hold my wonder now.
Yet, since you could not know, and it befell
That these are the last words your fingers wrote,
There is a dignity some might not see
In this, "I picked the first sweet-pea today."
Today! Was there an opening bud beside it
You left until tomorrow?—O my love,
The things that withered,—and you came not back!
That day you filled this circle of my arms

That now is empty. (O my empty life!)
That day—that day you picked the first sweet-pea,—
And brought it in to show me! I recall
With terrible distinctness how the smell
Of your cool gardens drifted in with you.
I know, you held it up for me to see
And flushed because I looked not at the flower,
But at your face; and when behind my look
You saw such unmistakable intent
You laughed and brushed your flower against my lips.
(You were the fairest thing God ever made,
I think.) And then your hands above my heart
Drew down its stem into a fastening,
And while your head was bent I kissed your hair.
I wonder if you knew. (Beloved hands!
Somehow I cannot seem to see them still.
Somehow I cannot seem to see the dust
In your bright hair.) What is the need of Heaven
When earth can be so sweet?—If only God
Had let us love,—and show the world the way!
Strange cancellings must ink th' eternal books
When love-crossed-out will bring the answer right!
That first sweet-pea! I wonder where it is.
It seems to me I laid it down somewhere,
And yet,—I am not sure. I am not sure,
Even, if it was white or pink; for then
'Twas much like any other flower to me,
Save that it was the first. I did not know,
Then, that it was the last. If I had known—
But then, it does not matter. Strange how few,
After all's said and done, the things that are
Of moment.

     Few indeed! When I can make
Of ten small words a rope to hang the world!
"I had you and I have you now no more."
There, there it dangles,—where's the little truth
That can for long keep footing under that
When its slack syllables tighten to a thought?
Here, let me write it down! I wish to see

Just how a thing like that will look on paper!

"*I had you and I have you now no more*."

O little words, how can you run so straight
Across the page, beneath the weight you bear?
How can you fall apart, whom such a theme
Has bound together, and hereafter aid
In trivial expression, that have been
So hideously dignified?—Would God
That tearing you apart would tear the thread
I strung you on! Would God—O God, my mind
Stretches asunder on this merciless rack
Of imagery! O, let me sleep a while!
Would I could sleep, and wake to find me back
In that sweet summer afternoon with you.
Summer? 'Tis summer still by the calendar!
How easily could God, if He so willed,
Set back the world a little turn or two!
Correct its griefs, and bring its joys again!

We were so wholly one I had not thought
That we could die apart. I had not thought
That I could move,—and you be stiff and still!
That I could speak,—and you perforce be dumb!
I think our heart-strings were, like warp and woof
In some firm fabric, woven in and out;
Your golden filaments in fair design
Across my duller fibre. And today
The shining strip is rent; the exquisite
Fine pattern is destroyed; part of your heart
Aches in my breast; part of my heart lies chilled
In the damp earth with you. I have been torn
In two, and suffer for the rest of me.
What is my life to me? And what am I
To life,—a ship whose star has guttered out?
A Fear that in the deep night starts awake
Perpetually, to find its senses strained
Against the taut strings of the quivering air,

Awaiting the return of some dread chord?

Dark, Dark, is all I find for metaphor;
All else were contrast,—save that contrast's wall
Is down, and all opposed things flow together
Into a vast monotony, where night
And day, and frost and thaw, and death and life,
Are synonyms. What now—what now to me
Are all the jabbering birds and foolish flowers
That clutter up the world? You were my song!
Now, let discord scream! You were my flower!
Now let the world grow weeds! For I shall not
Plant things above your grave—(the common balm
Of the conventional woe for its own wound!)
Amid sensations rendered negative
By your elimination stands today,
Certain, unmixed, the element of grief;
I sorrow; and I shall not mock my truth
With travesties of suffering, nor seek
To effigy its incorporeal bulk
In little wry-faced images of woe.

I cannot call you back; and I desire
No utterance of my immaterial voice.
I cannot even turn my face this way
Or that, and say, "My face is turned to you";
I know not where you are, I do not know
If Heaven hold you or if earth transmute,
Body and soul, you into earth again;
But this I know:—not for one second's space
Shall I insult my sight with visionings
Such as the credulous crowd so eager-eyed
Beholds, self-conjured, in the empty air.
Let the world wail! Let drip its easy tears!
My sorrow shall be dumb!

—What do I say?
God! God!—God pity me! Am I gone mad
That I should spit upon a rosary?

Am I become so shrunken? Would to God
I too might feel that frenzied faith whose touch
Makes temporal the most enduring grief;
Though it must walk a while, as is its wont,
With wild lamenting! Would I too might weep
Where weeps the world and hangs its piteous wreaths
For its new dead! Not Truth, but Faith, it is
That keeps the world alive. If all at once
Faith were to slacken,—that unconscious faith
Which must, I know, yet be the corner-stone
Of all believing,—birds now flying fearless
Across would drop in terror to the earth;
Fishes would drown; and the all-governing reins
Would tangle in the frantic hands of God
And the worlds gallop headlong to destruction!

O God, I see it now, and my sick brain
Staggers and swoons! How often over me
Flashes this breathlessness of sudden sight
In which I see the universe unrolled
Before me like a scroll and read thereon
Chaos and Doom, where helpless planets whirl
Dizzily round and round and round and round,
Like tops across a table, gathering speed
With every spin, to waver on the edge
One instant—looking over—and the next
To shudder and lurch forward out of sight—

\* \* \* \* \*

Ah, I am worn out—I am wearied out—
It is too much—I am but flesh and blood,
And I must sleep. Though you were dead again,
I am but flesh and blood and I must sleep.

# The Suicide

"Curse thee, Life, I will live with thee no more!
Thou hast mocked me, starved me, beat my body sore!

And all for a pledge that was not pledged by me,
I have kissed thy crust and eaten sparingly
That I might eat again, and met thy sneers
With deprecations, and thy blows with tears,—
Aye, from thy glutted lash, glad, crawled away,
As if spent passion were a holiday!
And now I go. Nor threat, nor easy vow
Of tardy kindness can avail thee now
With me, whence fear and faith alike are flown;
Lonely I came, and I depart alone,
And know not where nor unto whom I go;
But that thou canst not follow me I know."

Thus I to Life, and ceased; but through my brain
My thought ran still, until I spake again:

"Ah, but I go not as I came,—no trace
Is mine to bear away of that old grace
I brought! I have been heated in thy fires,
Bent by thy hands, fashioned to thy desires,
Thy mark is on me! I am not the same
Nor ever more shall be, as when I came.
Ashes am I of all that once I seemed.
In me all's sunk that leapt, and all that dreamed
Is wakeful for alarm,—oh, shame to thee,
For the ill change that thou hast wrought in me,
Who laugh no more nor lift my throat to sing!
Ah, Life, I would have been a pleasant thing
To have about the house when I was grown
If thou hadst left my little joys alone!
I asked of thee no favor save this one:
That thou wouldst leave me playing in the sun!
And this thou didst deny, calling my name
Insistently, until I rose and came.
I saw the sun no more.—It were not well
So long on these unpleasant thoughts to dwell,
Need I arise tomorrow and renew
Again my hated tasks, but I am through
With all things save my thoughts and this one night,

So that in truth I seem already quite
Free and remote from thee,—I feel no haste
And no reluctance to depart; I taste
Merely, with thoughtful mien, an unknown draught,
That in a little while I shall have quaffed."

Thus I to Life, and ceased, and slightly smiled,
Looking at nothing; and my thin dreams filed
Before me one by one till once again
I set new words unto an old refrain:

"Treasures thou hast that never have been mine!
Warm lights in many a secret chamber shine
Of thy gaunt house, and gusts of song have blown
Like blossoms out to me that sat alone!
And I have waited well for thee to show
If any share were mine,—and now I go!
Nothing I leave, and if I naught attain
I shall but come into mine own again!"
Thus I to Life, and ceased, and spake no more,
But turning, straightway, sought a certain door
In the rear wall. Heavy it was, and low
And dark,—a way by which none e'er would go
That other exit had, and never knock
Was heard thereat,—bearing a curious lock
Some chance had shown me fashioned faultily,
Whereof Life held content the useless key,
And great coarse hinges, thick and rough with rust,
Whose sudden voice across a silence must,
I knew, be harsh and horrible to hear,—
A strange door, ugly like a dwarf.—So near
I came I felt upon my feet the chill
Of acid wind creeping across the sill.
So stood longtime, till over me at last
Came weariness, and all things other passed
To make it room; the still night drifted deep
Like snow about me, and I longed for sleep.

But, suddenly, marking the morning hour,
Bayed the deep-throated bell within the tower!
Startled, I raised my head,—and with a shout
Laid hold upon the latch,—and was without.

\* \* \* \* \*

Ah, long-forgotten, well-remembered road,
Leading me back unto my old abode,
My father's house! There in the night I came,
And found them feasting, and all things the same
As they had been before. A splendour hung
Upon the walls, and such sweet songs were sung
As, echoing out of very long ago,
Had called me from the house of Life, I know.
So fair their raiment shone I looked in shame
On the unlovely garb in which I came;
Then straightway at my hesitancy mocked:
"It is my father's house!" I said and knocked;
And the door opened. To the shining crowd
Tattered and dark I entered, like a cloud,
Seeing no face but his; to him I crept,
And "Father!" I cried, and clasped his knees, and wept.
Ah, days of joy that followed! All alone
I wandered through the house. My own, my own,
My own to touch, my own to taste and smell,
All I had lacked so long and loved so well!
None shook me out of sleep, nor hushed my song,
Nor called me in from the sunlight all day long.

I know not when the wonder came to me
Of what my father's business might be,
And whither fared and on what errands bent
The tall and gracious messengers he sent.
Yet one day with no song from dawn till night
Wondering, I sat, and watched them out of sight.
And the next day I called; and on the third
Asked them if I might go,—but no one heard.
Then, sick with longing, I arose at last

And went unto my father,—in that vast
Chamber wherein he for so many years
Has sat, surrounded by his charts and spheres.
"Father," I said, "Father, I cannot play
The harp that thou didst give me, and all day
I sit in idleness, while to and fro
About me thy serene, grave servants go;
And I am weary of my lonely ease.
Better a perilous journey overseas
Away from thee, than this, the life I lead,
To sit all day in the sunshine like a weed
That grows to naught,—I love thee more than they
Who serve thee most; yet serve thee in no way.
Father, I beg of thee a little task
To dignify my days,—'tis all I ask
Forever, but forever, this denied,
I perish."

        "Child," my father's voice replied,
"All things thy fancy hath desired of me
Thou hast received. I have prepared for thee
Within my house a spacious chamber, where
Are delicate things to handle and to wear,
And all these things are thine. Dost thou love song?
My minstrels shall attend thee all day long.
Or sigh for flowers? My fairest gardens stand
Open as fields to thee on every hand.
And all thy days this word shall hold the same:
No pleasure shalt thou lack that thou shalt name.
But as for tasks—" he smiled, and shook his head;
"Thou hadst thy task, and laidst it by", he said.

## God's World

O world, I cannot hold thee close enough!
        Thy winds, thy wide grey skies!
        Thy mists, that roll and rise!
Thy woods, this autumn day, that ache and sag

And all but cry with colour! That gaunt crag
To crush! To lift the lean of that black bluff!
World, World, I cannot get thee close enough!

Long have I known a glory in it all,
        But never knew I this;
        Here such a passion is
As stretcheth me apart,—Lord, I do fear
Thou'st made the world too beautiful this year;
My soul is all but out of me,—let fall
No burning leaf; prithee, let no bird call.

## Afternoon on a Hill

I will be the gladdest thing
        Under the sun!
I will touch a hundred flowers
        And not pick one.

I will look at cliffs and clouds
        With quiet eyes,
Watch the wind bow down the grass,
        And the grass rise.

And when lights begin to show
        Up from the town,
I will mark which must be mine,
        And then start down!

## Sorrow

Sorrow like a ceaseless rain
        Beats upon my heart.
People twist and scream in pain,—
Dawn will find them still again;
This has neither wax nor wane,
 Neither stop nor start.

People dress and go to town;
 I sit in my chair.
All my thoughts are slow and brown:
Standing up or sitting down
Little matters, or what gown
 Or what shoes I wear.

## Tavern

I'll keep a little tavern
 Below the high hill's crest,
Wherein all grey-eyed people
 May set them down and rest.

There shall be plates a-plenty,
 And mugs to melt the chill
Of all the grey-eyed people
 Who happen up the hill.

There sound will sleep the traveller,
 And dream his journey's end,
But I will rouse at midnight
 The falling fire to tend.

Aye, 'tis a curious fancy—
 But all the good I know
Was taught me out of two grey eyes
 A long time ago.

## Ashes of Life

Love has gone and left me and the days are all alike;
 Eat I must, and sleep I will,—and would that night were here!
But ah!—to lie awake and hear the slow hours strike!
 Would that it were day again!—with twilight near!

Love has gone and left me and I don't know what to do;
     This or that or what you will is all the same to me;
But all the things that I begin I leave before I'm through,—
     There's little use in anything as far as I can see.

Love has gone and left me,—and the neighbors knock and borrow,
     And life goes on forever like the gnawing of a mouse,—
And tomorrow and tomorrow and tomorrow and tomorrow
     There's this little street and this little house.

# The Little Ghost

I knew her for a little ghost
     That in my garden walked;
The wall is high—higher than most—
     And the green gate was locked.

And yet I did not think of that
     Till after she was gone—
I knew her by the broad white hat,
     All ruffled, she had on.

By the dear ruffles round her feet,
     By her small hands that hung
In their lace mitts, austere and sweet,
     Her gown's white folds among.

I watched to see if she would stay,
     What she would do—and oh!
She looked as if she liked the way
     I let my garden grow!

She bent above my favourite mint
     With conscious garden grace,
She smiled and smiled—there was no hint
     Of sadness in her face.

She held her gown on either side
    To let her slippers show,
And up the walk she went with pride,
    The way great ladies go.

And where the wall is built in new
    And is of ivy bare
She paused—then opened and passed through
    A gate that once was there.

## Kin to Sorrow

Am I kin to Sorrow,
    That so oft
Falls the knocker of my door—
    Neither loud nor soft,
But as long accustomed,
    Under Sorrow's hand?
Marigolds around the step
    And rosemary stand,
And then comes Sorrow—
    And what does Sorrow care
For the rosemary
    Or the marigolds there?
Am I kin to Sorrow?
    Are we kin?
That so oft upon my door—
    *Oh, come in*!

# THREE SONGS OF SHATTERING

## I

The first rose on my rose-tree
    Budded, bloomed, and shattered,
During sad days when to me
        Nothing mattered.

Grief of grief has drained me clean;
    Still it seems a pity
No one saw,—it must have been
        Very pretty.

## II

Let the little birds sing;
    Let the little lambs play;
Spring is here; and so 'tis spring;—
    But not in the old way!

I recall a place
    Where a plum-tree grew;
There you lifted up your face,
    And blossoms covered you.

If the little birds sing,
    And the little lambs play,
Spring is here; and so 'tis spring—
 But not in the old way!

# III

All the dog-wood blossoms are underneath the tree!
    Ere spring was going—ah, spring is gone!
And there comes no summer to the like of you and me,—
    Blossom time is early, but no fruit sets on.

All the dog-wood blossoms are underneath the tree,
    Browned at the edges, turned in a day;
And I would with all my heart they trimmed a mound for me,
    And weeds were tall on all the paths that led that way!

## The Shroud

Death, I say, my heart is bowed
    Unto thine,—O mother!
This red gown will make a shroud
    Good as any other!

(I, that would not wait to wear
    My own bridal things,
In a dress dark as my hair
    Made my answerings.

I, tonight, that till he came
    Could not, could not wait,
In a gown as bright as flame
    Held for them the gate.)

Death, I say, my heart is bowed
    Unto thine,—O mother!
This red gown will make a shroud
    Good as any other!

# The Dream

Love, if I weep it will not matter,
    And if you laugh I shall not care;
Foolish am I to think about it,
    But it is good to feel you there.

Love, in my sleep I dreamed of waking,—
    White and awful the moonlight reached
Over the floor, and somewhere, somewhere,
    There was a shutter loose,—it screeched!

Swung in the wind,—and no wind blowing!—
    I was afraid, and turned to you,
Put out my hand to you for comfort,—
    And you were gone! Cold, cold as dew,

Under my hand the moonlight lay!
    Love, if you laugh I shall not care,
But if I weep it will not matter,—
    Ah, it is good to feel you there!

# Indifference

I said,—for Love was laggard, O, Love was slow to come,—
    "I'll hear his step and know his step when I am warm in bed;
But I'll never leave my pillow, though there be some
    As would let him in—and take him in with tears!" I said.
I lay,—for Love was laggard, O, he came not until dawn,—
    I lay and listened for his step and could not get to sleep;
And he found me at my window with my big cloak on,
    All sorry with the tears some folks might weep!

# Witch-Wife

She is neither pink nor pale,
    And she never will be all mine;
She learned her hands in a fairy-tale,
    And her mouth on a valentine.

She has more hair than she needs;
    In the sun 'tis a woe to me!
And her voice is a string of colored beads,
    Or steps leading into the sea.

She loves me all that she can,
    And her ways to my ways resign;
But she was not made for any man,
    And she never will be all mine.

# Blight

Hard seeds of hate I planted
    That should by now be grown,—
Rough stalks, and from thick stamens
    A poisonous pollen blown,
And odors rank, unbreathable,
    From dark corollas thrown!

At dawn from my damp garden
    I shook the chilly dew;
The thin boughs locked behind me
    That sprang to let me through;
The blossoms slept,—I sought a place
    Where nothing lovely grew.

And there, when day was breaking,
    I knelt and looked around:
The light was near, the silence
    Was palpitant with sound;

I drew my hate from out my breast
    And thrust it in the ground.

Oh, ye so fiercely tended,
    Ye little seeds of hate!
I bent above your growing
    Early and noon and late,
Yet are ye drooped and pitiful,—
    I cannot rear ye straight!

The sun seeks out my garden,
    No nook is left in shade,
No mist nor mold nor mildew
    Endures on any blade,
Sweet rain slants under every bough:
    Ye falter, and ye fade.

## When the Year Grows Old

I cannot but remember
    When the year grows old—
October—November—
    How she disliked the cold!

She used to watch the swallows
    Go down across the sky,
And turn from the window
    With a little sharp sigh.

And often when the brown leaves
    Were brittle on the ground,
And the wind in the chimney
    Made a melancholy sound,

She had a look about her
    That I wish I could forget—
The look of a scared thing
    Sitting in a net!

Oh, beautiful at nightfall
    The soft spitting snow!
And beautiful the bare boughs
    Rubbing to and fro!

But the roaring of the fire,
    And the warmth of fur,
And the boiling of the kettle
    Were beautiful to her!

I cannot but remember
    When the year grows old—
October—November—
    How she disliked the cold!

# SONNETS

## I

Thou art not lovelier than lilacs,—no,
    Nor honeysuckle; thou art not more fair
    Than small white single poppies,—I can bear
Thy beauty; though I bend before thee, though
From left to right, not knowing where to go,
    I turn my troubled eyes, nor here nor there
    Find any refuge from thee, yet I swear
So has it been with mist,—with moonlight so.

Like him who day by day unto his draught
    Of delicate poison adds him one drop more
Till he may drink unharmed the death of ten,
Even so, inured to beauty, who have quaffed
    Each hour more deeply than the hour before,
I drink—and live—what has destroyed some men.

## II

*I do hope that no one here has recently last a loved one*

Time does not bring relief; you all have lied
    Who told me time would ease me of my pain!
    I miss him in the weeping of the rain;
I want him at the shrinking of the tide;
The old snows melt from every mountain-side,
    And last year's leaves are smoke in every lane;
    But last year's bitter loving must remain
Heaped on my heart, and my old thoughts abide!

There are a hundred places where I fear
      To go,—so with his memory they brim!
And entering with relief some quiet place
Where never fell his foot or shone his face
I say, "There is no memory of him here!"
      And so stand stricken, so remembering him!

## III

Mindful of you the sodden earth in spring,
      And all the flowers that in the springtime grow,
      And dusty roads, and thistles, and the slow
Rising of the round moon, all throats that sing
The summer through, and each departing wing,
      And all the nests that the bared branches show,
      And all winds that in any weather blow,
And all the storms that the four seasons bring.

You go no more on your exultant feet
      Up paths that only mist and morning knew,
Or watch the wind, or listen to the beat
      Of a bird's wings too high in air to view,—
But you were something more than young and sweet
      And fair,—and the long year remembers you.

## IV

Not in this chamber only at my birth—
      When the long hours of that mysterious night
      Were over, and the morning was in sight—
I cried, but in strange places, steppe and firth
I have not seen, through alien grief and mirth;
      And never shall one room contain me quite
      Who in so many rooms first saw the light,
Child of all mothers, native of the earth.

So is no warmth for me at any fire
    Today, when the world's fire has burned so low;
I kneel, spending my breath in vain desire,
At that cold hearth which one time roared so strong,
And straighten back in weariness, and long
    To gather up my little gods and go.

V

If I should learn, in some quite casual way,
    That you were gone, not to return again—
Read from the back-page of a paper, say,
    Held by a neighbor in a subway train,
How at the corner of this avenue
    And such a street (so are the papers filled)
A hurrying man—who happened to be you—
    At noon today had happened to be killed,
I should not cry aloud—I could not cry
    Aloud, or wring my hands in such a place—
I should but watch the station lights rush by
    With a more careful interest on my face,
Or raise my eyes and read with greater care
Where to store furs and how to treat the hair.

VI

Bluebeard

This door you might not open, and you did;
    So enter now, and see for what slight thing
You are betrayed. . . . Here is no treasure hid,
    No cauldron, no clear crystal mirroring
The sought-for truth, no heads of women slain
    For greed like yours, no writhings of distress,
But only what you see. . . . Look yet again—
    An empty room, cobwebbed and comfortless.
Yet this alone out of my life I kept

Unto myself, lest any know me quite;
And you did so profane me when you crept
  Unto the threshold of this room tonight
That I must never more behold your face.
  This now is yours. I seek another place.


## VIII

Oh, oh, you will be sorry for that word!
Give back my book and take my kiss instead.
Was it my enemy or my friend I heard,
"What a big book for such a little head!"
Come, I will show you now my newest hat,
And you may watch me purse my mouth and prink!
Oh, I shall love you still, and all of that. *But n*
~~I never again shall tell you what I think~~.
I shall be sweet and crafty, soft and sly;
You will not catch me reading any more:
I shall be called a wife to pattern by;
And some day when you knock and push the door,
Some sane day, not too bright and not too stormy,
I shall be gone, and you may whistle for me.


## XVIII

I, being born a woman and distressed
By all the needs and notions of my kind,
Am urged by your propinquity to find
Your person fair, and feel a certain zest
To bear your body's weight upon my breast:
So subtly is the fume of life designed,
To clarify the pulse and cloud the mind,
And leave me once again undone, possessed.
Think not for this, however, the poor treason
Of my stout blood against my staggering brain,
I shall remember you with love, or season
My scorn with pity. -- let me make it plain:

I find this frenzy insufficient reason
For conversation when we meet again.

## IX

Here is a wound that never will heal, I know,
Being wrought not of a dearness and a death,
But of a love turned ashes and the breath
Gone out of beauty; never again will grow
The grass on that scarred acre, though I sow
Young seed there yearly and the sky bequeath
Its friendly weathers down, far underneath
Shall be such bitterness of an old woe.
That April should be shattered by a gust,
That August should be levelled by a rain,
I can endure, and that the lifted dust
Of man should settle to the earth again;
But that a dream can die, will be a thrust
Between my ribs forever of hot pain.

## XIX

What lips my lips have kissed, and where, and why,
I have forgotten, and what arms have lain
Under my head till morning; but the rain
Is full of ghosts to-night, that tap and sigh
Upon the glass and listen for reply,
And in my heart there stirs a quiet pain
For unremembered lads that not again
Will turn to me at midnight with a cry.
Thus in the winter stands the lonely tree,
Nor knows what birds have vanished one by one,
Yet knows its boughs more silent than before:
I cannot say what loves have come and gone,
I only know that summer sang in me
A little while, that in me sings no more.

* after a promiscuous life Millay perhaps
realises that in being so casual
with relationships she may end
up unloved and alone

Printed in the United Kingdom
by Lightning Source UK Ltd.
131564UK00001B/163/P